G Thomann

The Effects of Beer Upon Those Who Make and Drink it

G Thomann

The Effects of Beer Upon Those Who Make and Drink it

ISBN/EAN: 9783337142735

Printed in Europe, USA, Canada, Australia, Japan

Cover: Foto ©Andreas Hilbeck / pixelio.de

More available books at **www.hansebooks.com**

THE

EFFECTS OF BEER

UPON

THOSE WHO MAKE AND DRINK IT.

A STATISTICAL SKETCH

BY

G. THOMANN.

NEW YORK:

THE UNITED STATES BREWERS' ASSOCIATION.

1886.

EFFECTS OF BEER

THOSE WHO MAKE AND DRINK IT.

"The constant use of beer is found to produce a species of degeneration of
.st of the organism, profound and very deceptive. Fatty deposits, dimin-
ished circulation, congestions, general disturbances of the functions of the
different organs, inflammation of both the liver and kidney, are, one or all,
constantly present." *

The foregoing extract from a text-book on physiology is a
typical specimen of the absurdities with which biased or ignorant
teachers are permitted to fill the heads of school-children. Very
many writers and public lecturers, unless they derive their
information directly from one of the many self-constituted medical authorities, unknown beyond the limits of the hamlets in
which they minister to science, make use of just such groundless
and absurd averments in order to prove that beer is an unwholesome beverage.

If what is claimed in this quotation be true, there ought to
be no difficulty in producing medical statistics in support of it.
But no such proof has ever been produced, for the very simple
reason that it does not exist. In the absence of statistical testimony, an assertion like that quoted might be accepted as the
individual opinion of a medical practitioner; and as such would
deserve as much credence as the practitioner's reputation for pro-
fessional skill, exactness of observation and incorruptibility of
judgment might warrant. But in our case, not even this much
can be admitted, because methodical investigations, conducted by
institutions of learning and the governments of many countries,
have taken the matter out of the domain of empiricism and specu-

---

* Lessons on the human body ; by O. M. Brands.

lation, by scientifically and statistically establishing the fact that beer *is* a wholesome beverage.

Long before these investigations were undertaken, however, this fact was generally known; and the student of history would find it an easy task to adduce proof of its having been well appreciated. In all ages beer-drinking nations have been remarkable for unusual intrepidity, great strength, vigor and vitality. It was not until after the introduction of ardent spirits into England, that the enervation of the masses was spoken of in connection with intemperate drinking-habits. The proceedings of the first Congress of the United States, and the state papers submitted to that body, prove that the most eminent among the founders of our republic appreciated what was then styled "*the moralizing tendency and salubrious nature* of fermented liquors." In 1789, the legislature of Massachusetts passed an act encouraging the manufacture of beer for the reason—set forth in the preamble—that the "*wholesome qualities of malt liquors greatly recommend them to general use as an important means of preserving the health of the citizens.*" In colonial days, long before Dr. Rush began his agitation in favor of beer, the law-makers strove by all means at their command to popularize beer for sanitary reasons. When, in 1759, parliament had under consideration the proposition to re-enact a law of the preceding session, prohibiting malt distillation, petitions were received from the mayors and aldermen of nearly all the larger cities of Great Britain, London among them, setting forth that the law, which they begged to have re-enacted, had "produced the happiest consequences upon the morals, behavior, industry and *health* of the lower classes," by winning them back to the use of malt-liquors. Such evidences might be multiplied at will. But they would not be to the point in the present undertaking

It is known that alcoholism is a modern disease, and that methodical enquiry and observation were not directed to the effects of intoxicating drinks upon the human mind and body until after the ravages of alcoholism—acknowledged by all medical writers of repute to be the result of the excessive use of distilled spirits—had attracted the attention of the statesmen and lawmakers.

Now let us see what the results of these enquiries and observations are.

5

In Belgium, temperance societies, aided by the government and the Académie royal de médicine de Belgique, investigated the effects of the different intoxicating beverages upon the health of the masses, and came to the conclusion that the use of beer, being in every way a perfectly wholesome drink, ought to be encouraged by proper fiscal legislation. While waiting for such legislation, these temperance societies erected model breweries ; and offered prizes and promised their patronage and support to brewers who would brew beer of the quality-standard established by them.

The Académie de médicine of Paris, through its most eminent members, inaugurated a movement in favor of the encouragement of the brewing industry in France ; and such scientists as Lancereaux, Marvaud, Pasteur, and Bourchardat, after having scientifically investigated the matter, are now engaged in the work of convincing the French people that beer is an excellent drink, possessing many qualities that contribute to the health of those who use it. The plan of action of these scientific temperance advocates was officially stated by Dr. Lancereaux at the recent International Temperance Congress held at Antwerp. It culminates in the determination to have all taxes removed from the manufacture and sale of beer. And all this in the face of the fact, that viticulture forms an essential part of the wealth of France.

The medical inquiries made in Holland led to the conclusion that beer is an entirely healthy beverage ; and as early as 1877 the organ of the French temperance societies, *La Tempérance*, reported, that the object of the Dutch sister societies was, " de dégrever autant que possible la biére indigène," that is, to render domestic beer as free as possible from taxation.

The question of combating alcoholism was not discussed anywhere with more thoroughness than in Switzerland. The Federal legislature, the entire executive machinery, the statistical bureau, the sanitary commissions, the inspectors of factories, in short, all branches of the Federal and cantonal governments were engaged in the solution of this great question. Everything that pertains to the life of the people was looked into. Their food, their common drink, their dwellings, their social habits, their occupations ; in short, all things that could in any manner throw light upon the subject, were investigated. The material collected during these protracted enquiries covers, in small type, over two thousand 12mo pages. The outcome of it is, that the government assumes monopoly and rigid control of distillation and strives by proper fiscal legislation to encourage the use of beer, which the investigation proved to be a perfectly healthy drink, the general use of which, according to the printed opinion of the Swiss statistical bureau, would be regarded as a blessing to that country.

In Sweden, Denmark and Norway, like investigations produced similar results. A British select commission, in 1852, thoroughly investigated the drink-question, with special reference to the use of malt-liquors, and reported that they found beer to be a perfectly wholesome drink.

In our country we have, so far, at least one reliable collection of data on the subject; namely, that which was submitted by a sanitary commission, appointed by President Lincoln to examine the camps of the Union army and report upon their sanitary condition. In examining the condition of regiments in which malt-liquors were freely used, said commission found not only that beer is a healthy beverage, but that it possesses hygienic qualities which recommend its use for the prevention of certain diseases.

To be brief, wherever the effects of the use of beer upon the human body have been examined methodically by competent physicians, it was found—to use the words of Dr. Jules Rochard, of the Académie de médecine of Paris—that beer is a very healthy beverage, which helps digestion, quenches thirst and furnishes an amount of assimilable substances much greater than that contained in any other beverage

There is not the slightest statistical evidence to invalidate this assertion; and hence our conclusion must be, that it requires an uncommon degree either of ignorance or of mendacity to claim that beer produces the diseases enumerated in our introductory quotation; or that the rate of mortality among beer-drinkers is greater than among any other class of people.

A number of shrewd writers, who are but too well aware of the utter futility of any attempt to controvert the overwhelming medical testimony in favor of beer; but who, nevertheless, for reasons best known to themselves, wish to make their readers believe that the use of beer is dangerous to the health, resort to a artifice which, until recently, might have misled the ignorant and credulous. While they admit that pure beer is harmless, they either insinuate or openly charge that American beer of the present day is composed of poisonous ingredients that cannot but injure the health of the drinker.

As a specimen of this sort of misrepresentation, I quote the following from an article in the *North American Review*, of September 1886, written by Petroleum V. Nasby :

Lager beer **was originally** a seductive fluid, **a mild-mannered demon, as** innocent in appearance as spring water, and as beautiful. There are but few things on earth more beautiful than lager beer. The rich color in the glass, the liquid itself as clear as water, with its delicate amber tint, surmounted with the creamy foam overtopping it, is a **very** pretty sight, **and one which appeals** strongly **to the lust** of the eye. And then its taste ! The delicate, sweetish bitter is wonderfully grateful, and, when cold as ice, the taste lingers lovingly on the palate, the warmth cheers the stomach, and it is as refreshing a drink as man could wish. *And in justice it must be said that the lager beer of thirty years ago was comparatively harmless.* Then it was made of nothing but malt and hops, it was "laid" for nearly a **year** until it had undergone all the fermentations, and it could be taken, in moderate quantities, safely. Lager beer originally contained **only three or four per cent.** of alcohol, but it now contains ten and twelve per cent. The original beer did not make drunkards fast enough. It took too long a time **to fix the habit** so as **to make the victim profitable.** Hence they threw in glucose to make more alcohol, *and all sorts of cheap drugs of the maddening kind,* that the drinker might be bound hand and foot, and put into their possession in an absolutely helpless condition as soon as possible. It was not enough to make a beer-drinker of him—to get the largest profit it became necessary to *make a drunkard of him.* It resulted as anticipated.

The editor of the *North American Review* may have had good reasons for permitting his contributor to accuse the American brewers of adulteration ; but these reasons, whatever they may have been, could not convince the public that Mr. Nasby told the truth, and that the members of the State Board of Health of New York—who, in pursuance of law, had four hundred and seventy-six samples of malt liquors analyzed—told a falsehood, when they announced officially that all analyzed beers were found to be perfectly pure and wholesome, and to contain neither hop-substitutes nor any deleterious substances whatever. *

* It is worthy of note that whenever the charge of adulteration was brought against brewers in such manner as to lead to governmental investigations, the result has always been like that recently published by the N. Y. Health Board. In 1852, a select commission of the British parliament investigated such charges made against eleven of the largest breweries in England and found, to use their own words: "that no deleterious ingredients have been used by any of the eleven great breweries ; * * * that the charge so far as it was intended to be pointed at the eleven great breweries, is, with the above single exception, unfounded." The single exception was that of a brewer who, many years before the investigation, had used cream of tartar to neutralize the excessive acidity of a quantity of beer.

If in the face of such figures and facts as those presented by the said Board of Health, the editor of a periodical of the standing of the *North American Review* dares to publish articles of the Nasby calibre, it is not to be wondered at that the influence of so-called temperance advocates succeeded in *inducing one or two life-insurance companies* to declare publicly that the insuring of the lives of habitual beer-drinkers involved too many extra risks to be advisable. Nor is it wonderful that, coming from such a source, this declaration is regarded as the outcome of systematic investigations made by competent physicians.

It is this deceptive appearance of a statistical foundation that lent undue weight to the statement of these insurance companies, and called for more than an off-hand reply.

The first step which had to be taken in this matter, in order to get at the whole truth, was to ascertain whether the examining physicians of any life-insurance company had collected statistics showing that the constant or excessive use of beer causes an abnormal rate of mortality. Diligent enquiry failed to disclose any indications justifying the assumption that an attempt had ever been made in this direction. At all events, no statistics of the nature described could be found in insurance circles. And this was to be expected; for the fact is that, if statistical material of this kind existed at all, it could not, in the nature of things, have been collected by life-insurance companies through their examining physicians in this special capacity. These physicians are able, no doubt, to ascertain the actual state of health of persons brought before them for examination; but that is all they can know. They know nothing of the past condition, previous state of health, mode of life and habits of the applicant, except what the latter may tell them; and in this respect all depends upon the memory, intelligence and good-will of the person examined. When the examination is finished and the applicant insured, the physician hears no more of him, save by chance. If the insured person dies, the insurance company's physician can ascertain what disease is supposed to have caused the decease; but he can know nothing of the origin of the disease, and he is unable to say, whether there were contributive causes, latent predisposition or complicating ailments; or whether, and to what extent, the habits and mode of life of the deceased, or the medical treatment which he received, aggravated the malady and accelerated dissolution.

No more need be said to demonstrate the absurdity of the claim, that the experiences of life-insurance companies, and the observations made by their examining physicians in the discharge of their official duties, could throw any light on the effects of malt-liquors upon the human body. These physicians might, most assuredly, institute an investigation of this kind; but in the line of enquiry that would have to be pursued in that case, their experiences as examining physicians of life-insurance companies would be of no avail. They would have to follow the course marked out by the Swiss and Belgian governments and the French academicians. In doing so, they would not, of course, find any statistics in support of the absurd assertion that beer is an unwholesome drink; but they would get at the truth in an unerring manner. Conclusions arrived at in this way are firm as rocks. For instance, when the Swiss government, finding that alcoholism is unknown in localities where beer is the common drink, and that the people there are robust and long-lived, concludes that beer is a healthy drink—who would have the hardihood to gainsay such a conclusion? When it is found that recruits for military service (annually examined by the thousands), who were nurtured on beer and imbibe great quantities of that liquid every day, are perfect pictures of health; strong, vigorous, sound in every way—what conclusion can be admitted but that beer is a wholesome beverage?

Conclusions still more convincing than those cited, by way of illustration, might be obtained by comparing the physical condition of beer-drinking nations with that of nations commonly using other drinks; and in this particular I might present statistics taken from European and American censuses, state and federal, that would silence the most skeptical. But I have something far better to offer, and here it is.

About five years ago the brewers of New York, Brooklyn, Newark and the neighboring towns and villages established what they call a Benevolent Bureau for the relief of their sick and disabled employees, and for assisting the families of deceased brewery workmen. Every workman belonging to the B. B. pays a fixed sum into the relief-fund; and every employer contributes a sum equal to the total amount of dues paid by his employees. The different cities, having breweries which form part of this institution, are divided into medical districts, for which physicians in good standing are appointed by **the officers of** the Bureau. It is the duty of these physicians to **visit all sick** members, and to certify over their signatures, whether, **under** existing rules and regulations, the patient is entitled to the stipulated pecuniary assistance. Records of all cases of sickness and of all deaths are kept by the secretary of the Bureau, to whom the physicians send monthly reports setting forth, among other things, the names of patients and the nature of the ailments, in case of sickness; and of the cause in case of death.

In the course of time these physicians obtained almost a monopoly of medical practice among brewery workmen, and thus became thoroughly familiar with the physical condition of the men. Their official reports together with their every-day observations **would in** themselves suffice to form a basis—scientific and statistical—for a complete refutation of the absurd assertions in **reference to** malt-liquors. But, while it is not intended to waste **such** excellent material, **it** would be unwise to rest our case upon **it** exclusively, seeing **that** through the **instrumentality** of this conscientiously conducted institution, **with its competent** medical staff, **we are** enabled to present the outcome of just **such an investigation as** I advised insurance companies to institute, if **they would** know what **the effects** of the constant **use** of malt-liquors really **are.**

Before **proceeding to** a consideration **of the** showing of this investigation, **let us look** into a few statistical exhibits, compiled from the monthly reports **of** the physicians.

The largest medical **district** and the **one** having the greatest **number of** brewery workmen belonging to the Benevolent Bureau, **is that of** Dr. Guido Katzenmayer. The **number** of men under his medical care varies between nine hundred and one thousand, **the average** number being 960. In his **report on** special **examinations,** appended to this, **he** accounts **for 803** men, exclusive of **the men** employed in **the** breweries of **P.** Dölger, P. Buckel, **J.** Ahles, **J.** Dölger and Schmitt & Schwanenflügel, all of whom belong to his district, but were **not** examined, 1., because **it was not** intended **to have** more than **one** thousand men **on** the lists prepared for our special purpose; and, 2., because **it** was thought proper to include at least **one** other district in **this** investigation besides Dr. Katzenmayer's.

Dr. Katzenmayer **assumed** medical charge **of** this district in

November 1881, and continues up to the present day to discharge the **duties** of visiting and examining physician.

From his monthly reports, covering a period **of** *five* years, it appears that, in the aggregate, *thirty-six deaths occurred* **in** *his district; that is to say, that about seven deaths occurred annually* **in** a district having between nine hundred **and one thousand** workmen constantly employed in breweries. As I have shown, the system of medical supervision, the manner of recording casualties, together with the mode of controlling the expenditures of the Benevolent Bureau, leave no room for guess-work in this connection. All statements here made are matters of record, open to everybody's inspection.

The **following list shows, in the** given order, the names of the deceased, **the names of the brewers** by whom they have been employed, **and the cause of death:**

Name of Deceased.	Brewery.	Cause.
John Stiehl	G. Winter	Accident.
John Pfefferle	H. Clausen B. Co.	"
J. Kazmaier	G. Ehret	Cirrhosis of liver.
Val. Kauff	J. Kress B. Co.	Accident.
J. Deckelmann	H. Schalk	Bright's disease.
Hy. Diehl	F. & M. Schæfer B. Co.	Rupture of Heart.
Dan. Schankwecker	G. Ringler & Co.	Typhoid fever.
Geo. Kreissel	P. Dölger	Apoplexy.
Matth. Schleicher	Hy. Clausen B. Co.	Cerebral congestion.
Rob. Sommer	J. Ruppert	Pneumonia.
A. Heintzmann	H. Clausen B. Co.	Tuberculosis of lungs.
M. Hinzelberger	J. Ruppert	Apoplexy.
Wm. Moser	G. Ringler & Co.	Chronic enteritis.
Geo. Fuerst	J. Ruppert	Heart disease.
Louis Seffrich	G. Ehret	Typhoid fever.
Geo. Sauter	"	Insolation.
Rob. Kawinski	P. Dölger	Heart disease.
Gust. Behrmann	H. Clausen B. Co.	Apoplexy.
E. von Lilienthal	F. Oppermann, Jr.	Tuberculosis of lungs.
M. Siebenhändel	H. Clausen B. Co.	" " "
M. Wernert	G. Ehret	" " "
John Schwartz	G. Ringler & Co.	Pneumonia.
Matth. Biebl	F. Oppermann, Jr.	"
Mich. Hannelly	J. Ruppert	Drowned.
John Niessen	H. Clausen B. Co.	Alcoholism.
Th. Garter	" "	Accident.
Ferdinand Daub	P. Dölger	Pneumonia.
Ch. Kiefer	J. Ruppert	Paralysis of heart.

Name of Deceased.	*Brewery.*	*Cause.*
Matth. Gerber............J. Ruppert............		Carcinomata of liver and stomach.
Wm. Reinisch..........P. Dölger.............		Typhoid fever.
Christ Mahler ....G. Ehret.............		Carcinoma of liver.
Geo. Schreiber..........P. Dölger............		Cerebral congestion.
Carl Abt................ "		Typhoid fever.
Wm. Dirkes.............G. Ringler & Co......		Apoplexy.
John Winheim ....P. Dölger............		Tuberculosis of lungs.
John Pfauth............H. Clausen B. Co........		Cirrhosis of liver.

Recapitulating the casualties that occurred in said district
during five years, we find that there were:

```
Deaths caused by accidents .............................   5
   "      "   apoplexy and cerebral congestion..........   6
   "    · "   tuberculosis of lungs...................   5
   "      "   typhoid fever........................   4
   "      "   pneumonia.....  ......  .............   4
   "      "   diseases of the heart..........:.............·   4
   "      "     "     "   liver.....................   4
   "      "     "     "   kidneys...................   1
   "      "   insolation ...............................   1
   "      "   alcoholism............. ......  .........   1
   "      "   chronic enteritis............  .............   1
                                                       ───
                  Total.............................  36
```

The only case of alcoholism on record invited a special enquiry
into the drinking-habits of the person in question, and it was
found that in the last three or four years of his life the deceased
had been addicted to the excessive use of ardent spirits. This
case of alcoholism—a rare one among brewery workmen of any
country—stood isolated not only on the list of deaths, but also, as
will presently be seen, on the sick-lists from the districts investigated. Of diseases of the heart, liver and kidneys, the recapitu-
lation shows *nine* in all; that is to say, nine deaths occurred from
diseases of that class, within five years, in a body of nine hundred
and sixty brewery workmen. From disease of the kidneys but
one man died within five years. If, in conjunction with this
showing, it is stated that the average daily consumption of malt-
liquors by brewery workmen is twenty-five common glasses, or
about ten pints, *per capita*, no more need be said, it is hoped, to
disprove the assertion that the constant use of beer disorders,
with fatal effect, the functions of the heart, kidneys, and liver.

Before comparing the death-rate among brewery workmen with the pertinent mortuary statistics contained in the United States census for 1880, it is necessary to state that such a comparison must inevitably be very favorable to any one who intends to assail my position, because the benefit of doubt and of the inevitable inaccuracies of so gigantic a work as the census will be on his side, not on mine. To begin with, he will have an advantage over me in that the mortality report of the census (so far as it is at present accessible*) does not, according to the admission of its compiler, include all the deaths that occurred within the year covered by it; while the mortuary report submitted here, by a physician of the Benevolent Bureau, is absolutely accurate. Here, then, the rate of death is given correctly; while in the census it is reported as being lower than it actually was. In addition to this, the fact should be considered that the statistical information given in the census report on mortality relates to the entire population, including the rich, the wealthy, and the well-to-do, to whom, so far as the death-rate is concerned, the small pauper element of our country forms no offset; while the statistical showing herein contained relates to one single specified class of craftsmen. This is a difference which, the impartial critic must admit, is not in my favor in the case of the proposed comparison. Now let us compare figures.

The number of deaths in our body of 960 brewery workmen was 36, within five years; hence the average number of deaths within one year was 7.2. This places the rate of death per thousand at 7.5. The ages of these brewery workmen range, in varying proportions, from 19 to 59 years. The only rates of death, contained in Vol. XI of the census, that can fairly be brought into a comparison with the foregoing showing, will be found in Table 6, page xxv, which shows for the United States and for thirty-one registration cities "the proportion of deaths, in the different groups of ages, per 1,000 living." Of this table only that portion can properly be reproduced here for comparison, which covers the "groups of ages" represented in our showing, and, of course, only the figures

---

* The able compiler of this report, Dr. Billings, refers in Part I to just such tables as would be of value here, as being contained in Part II. In answer to an enquiry, Mr. Geo. M. Lockwood, Chief Clerk of the Interior Department, telegraphed under date of December 13, 1886: " Volume XII, Part II of mortality report is now going through the press."

relating to the urban population will answer the present purpose.
They are given as follows:

Ages.	Proportion of deaths to 1,000 living.	Ages.	Proportion of deaths to 1,000 living.
20–25	8.5	35–40	14.0
25–30	10.3	45–50	17.6
30–35	11.3	50–55	19.2

It might be said that these figures, so far as ages are concerned,
do not correspond exactly with the figures of the Brewer's Benevolent Bureau, because they begin at 20 instead of 19, and end at
55 instead of 59. The disparity, which is unavoidable on account
of the mode of grouping ages adopted by the census officials,
operates against the objects of this pamphlet; seeing that the
rate of death per 1,000 between 15 and 20 is only 5.5; while between 55 and 60 it is 28.3. The aggregate of living population
in the above six groups of ages was 3,333,878; the total number
of deaths 41,601; hence the rate of death per 1,000, within the
stated age-limits, was 12.5.

It is clear, then, that instead of involving extra risks, the insuring of the lives of habitual beer-drinkers must be more than
ordinarily profitable to insurance companies, since the chances of
loss in this special case are to the general risks as 7.5 is to 12.5.
In other words, the risks incurred in insuring the lives of
habitual beer-drinkers are less, by forty per cent., than the ordinary
risks of such transactions.

The death-rate in the regular army of the United States during the fiscal year 1885—a year of peace, in which, as the Surgeon
General's report states, no casualties from actual warfare were
returned—was 10.9 per 1,000 of mean strength. Medical examinations at recruiting stations for the regular military service are
conducted with a special view to securing men of good physique,
of great strength and perfect health. Besides, as compared with
the life of a brewery workman, with its hard and steady work
and manifold cares, the soldier's life in peace is an easy one. Excepting such accidents as are inseparable from the constant hand-
ling of fire-arms, the soldier, in times of peace, is exposed to fewer
chances of disease and death than the average workman. Well-
fed, comfortably quartered and clothed, he lives without cares or
troubles, in a constant routine of healthful exercise. Yet, even
as compared with the soldier in peace-time, we find that the

brewery workmen have a great advantage in point of low rate of mortality. It is true, the deaths from accidents were uncommonly numerous in the army, their proportion to the deaths from all other causes being given at 31 per cent.; that is more than again as large as the ratio of deaths from accidents among brewery workmen. But even so, the difference in favor of the latter is remarkable. The number of deaths in the army was 263 from all causes; the number of deaths from accidents was 83, in a body of soldiers of an average strength of 24,035. Deducting that number of deaths from accidents, which is in excess of the proportion returned for brewery workmen, we still have 46 more deaths, in a total of 263, than would have occurred at the rate of death among brewery workmen.—So much for the claim that the insuring of the lives of habitual beer-drinkers involves extra risks.

Compiling the monthly reports and sick-lists rendered by Dr. Katzenmayer during five years, and classifying the causes of sickness in the usual general way, the relative proportion of the various diseases treated by said physician, during the period covered by his reports, is found to be as follows:

42.9 per cent. of surgical cases caused by accidents of all kinds, fractures, dislocations, contusions, wounds, etc.
27.5 " " " disturbances of the alimentary canal, acute catarrh of the stomach, intestinal catarrh, diarrhœa, dysentery, etc.
12.5 " " " rheumatic diseases.
9.4 " " " diseases of the air passages: tonsilletis, diphtheria, bronchitis, pneumonia, pleuresy, etc.
3.6 " " " fevers; typhoid, intermittent, etc.
2.1 " " " acute congestions of liver and kidneys.
1.0 " " " diseases of the skin.
0.6 " " " cerebral and spinal diseases.
0.4 " " " diseases of the heart.

Considered in conjunction with what has already been said and proved as to diseases of a certain order, the foregoing figures are too eloquent *per se*, to need further elucidation.

If no other data could be obtained, the showing thus far presented might be made to answer all purposes of a controversy with opponents who have neither statistical nor historical proofs to offer for their assertions. But, as has already been said, the existence of a sort of brewers' insurance company, with a complete medical staff, suggested the advisability of instituting a special investigation with exclusive reference to the effects of malt-liquors upon the human body.

It will readily be admitted by everybody that among the entire population of the United States not another body of men of equal number could be found, who, from their mode of life and drinking-habits, would be better suited for such a purpose than brewery workmen. For, as a class, they drink beer and ale more constantly and more copiously than the average beer-drinker. For the information of those who are not acquainted with the usages prevailing in breweries, it must be stated that brewery workmen have at all times access to what in the jargon of the trade is styed the "Sternenwirth," *i. e.*, a room, set apart within every brew-house, where beer is constantly "on tap," to be used by every one at pleasure and *without cost*. Every one drinks as much beer as he thirsts for, without asking or being asked any questions as to his right to do so.

These brewery workmen are a body of men who, on the days when they turn out in force for their annual out-door festivals, attract much attention by their stalwart physique, their healthy appearance and the noticeable rarity of that obesity, which is popularly but erroneously supposed to be a result of the use of malt-liquors; but which, in the case of a certain class of easy-going and well-to-do Germans, is attributable to a number of things that, together, make up a peculiar mode of life. As to the condition of these men in point of wages, work and habits (important factors in every way) a few words must be said, especially because the United States Census for 1880 (Vol. XX, Statistics of wages) contains but very little information on that subject, and that little relating only to six breweries in small western towns. The lowest weekly wages (excepting those of apprentices at $10) paid in the breweries of New York—the city to which all our figures refer—are those of workmen in wash-houses and engine-rooms. These men receive $15 per week; brewers at work in cellars, fermenting rooms and at kettles receive $18 per week. All men work twelve hours, that is to say they are engaged from 6 A. M. to 6 P. M., but within that time they have two hours of leisure for meals. The nature of their work requires physical strength, but does not exhaust the energies by reason of undue or continued tension. The proportion of married men is very large. Their food is simple, but, as a rule, substantial and very judiciously chosen. In point of education and intellect they are much above the average, illiteracy being very rare among them. Their social habits are those of the average German-American workmen—simple, pure, and as far removed from licentiousness as from asceticism.

With a view to ascertaining, in the most reliable manner possible, the effects of the use of malt-liquors, the physicians of the Benevolent Bureau examined one thousand of these men, engaged in breweries, as to: 1, general state of health; 2, condition of liver; 3, condition of kidneys; 4, condition of heart. In addition to this, the physicians were directed to weigh and measure every man; to test his strength by dynamometer; state his age, length of time employed in breweries, and average daily quantity of beer consumed.

By referring to the appended tables it will be found that the initials of the name of every man* and the name of his employer are given, so that any physician inclined to verify the results of our examinations will have no trouble in doing so.

These examinations showed, that there are, in all, twenty-five men out of one thousand, whose general state of health, or condition of liver, or condition of heart, or condition of kidneys, is not perfect; and that the remaining nine hundred and seventy-five men enjoy exceptionally good health, and are of splendid physique. The average daily consumption of malt-liquors is 25.73 glasses, about 10 pints, *per capita*.

Of the twenty-five men recorded as unsound, a very large proportion would not have been so returned in our tables, if the examinations had been confined to the condition of the heart, the liver and the kidneys. But it was thought necessary to point out all those whose health is impaired from any cause whatever; no matter, whether the latter can be traced to the use of beer or not. Hence, when the "general state of health" was found, in any case, to be precarious, the physician had to make a corresponding entry in his list and explain the same under the head of special remarks by stating the cause or nature of the infirmity. This accounts for the fact that such diseases as icterus, bronchitis, rheumatism, tuberculosis of lungs, etc., are specified as causes impairing the "general state of health."

* The full names of the men examined are inscribed on a list in the hands of the examiners, and can be referred to as a guide to the appended tables.

Dividing the twenty-five unsound men according to the nature of diseases which impaired their health, we obtain the following:

Diseases of the liver	7
" " heart	1
" " kidneys	5
Emphysema	1
Rheumatism	6
Icterus	2
Bronchitis	2
Tuberculosis of lungs	1

The causes of the three first-named diseases are known to be so manifold, that it would be more than venturesome to assume, in the off-hand way of our opponents, that beer is at the bottom of them all. Yet no attempt will be made to weaken the showing as it stands, save in the case of Ch. W. (230) whose ailment, abscess of liver, was produced, to the positive knowledge of the physicians who performed an operation on the patient, by external injuries.

Rheumatism and diseases of the air passages are generally regarded by brewers as their trade diseases, produced either by constant exposure to the inclemency of the weather, as in the case of drivers; or by exposure to the sudden and extreme changes of temperature incident to the work in cellars, ice-houses and cooling-rooms; or by exposure to the constant moisture in wash-houses.

An adequate basis for comparing the results of our examination with the prevalence of the diseases named in other portions of the population, is not at hand. It is assumed, however, that what has before been shown, will suffice for all practical purposes.

As a rule, the men examined displayed unusual muscular strength. The average weight lifted was 480 pounds; the lowest weight indicated on the dynamometer, used by Dr. Katzenmayer, being 390 pounds. Grouping the men according to the length of time they are employed in breweries, we find the largest number in the group from five to ten years, there being about 300 in it. From ten to fifteen years the number is 187, and from fifteen to twenty 122. Those who are engaged in brewing from one month to two years are a little more numerous than those who were thus engaged for over twenty, and less than twenty-five years. The number of men at work over twenty-five years is 46. In the first and last groups no unsound men were found; in the other groups the numbers are as follows:

	Number of Men.	Average daily quantity of beer consumed per capita.
From 2 to 5 years,	2	23.62
" 5 " 10 "	4	24.63
" 10 " 15 "	6	26.60
" 15 " 20 "	5	26.09
" 20 " 25 "	8	26.22

Comparing height of body and breadth of chest with the weight (see columns 5, 6, 7 and 8 of our tables) it will be found that, as a rule, brewery workmen, as has already been said, are not remarkable for obesity; on the contrary, the rare occurrence of weight that does not correspond with the size of the men is striking. It is reasonable to assume that the mode of life of brewery workmen accounts for this favorable showing, and that the same quantities of beer, if consumed by men of sedentary habits—shoemakers, for example—would produce different results. The error made by nearly all writers on this subject arises from a misconception as to the difference between a constant and an excessive use of malt-liquors. The nature of the work in which men are engaged and the general manner of living determine the quantities of malt-liquors men can consume without injury to their healths. It is a fact well known to every one who has devoted any attention to this matter, that the daily consumption of beer among Germans, the majority of whom are habitual, but not excessive beer-drinkers, varies from five to twenty glasses, according to the nature of the occupation of the drinker.

In the case of the brewery workmen, surroundings and usage favor the consumption of *unusually* large quantities of beer; yet, as we have seen, both as to immunity from disease, and low rate of mortality, this very class of workmen enjoy marked advantages. Here, then, the use of malt-liquors, despite the large quantities habitually consumed, cannot be deemed excessive; but might, and probably would, be regarded as such, if indulged in to the same extent by men of sedentary habits. And in the latter case the health of the drinkers might be impaired in consequence of such copious use, just as a quantity of meat, barely sufficient to appease the hunger of an agricultural laborer, would disorder the stomach of a man of different habits, engaged in a calling that requires no physical exertion. Nothing, it appears, is more difficult than to establish a general limit to quantity, beyond which the use of malt-liquors may properly be styled excessive. But whatever the quantity consumed by a man may be, we can not regard it as excessive so long as the man's health is not affected by it. When, in spite of the constant consumption of large quantities of malt-liquors, we find that the health of the drinkers is unusually good, the rate of mortality among them uncommonly low, and longevity above the average,* we must conclude not only that malt-liquors are wholesome beverages, but that their use in the quantities stated in our table is not injurious to the health of hard-working persons. This is what our examinations demonstrate in the most convincing manner.

Before concluding, it may not be amiss to direct attention to the condition of those men who worked in breweries over twenty years. In not a few instances, the vigor displayed by these men, and the entire absence of bodily ailments, past or present, surprised even the examining physicians. Such a case as that given in our list opposite No. 837 (G. W.) ought to convince the most sceptical, that beer is a wholesome drink. Here is a man of 56 years of age, uninterruptedly at work in breweries during 32 years, who drank beer throughout this time at the rate of 50 glasses per day; yet has never been sick, and to-day is perfectly healthy, vigorous and active. He is not an exception; our tables exhibit many cases like this.†

What the statistics herein presented demonstrate with absolute accuracy, may be summed up, then, in these words:

I. Brewers drink more beer, and drink it more constantly, than any other class of people.

II. The rate of death among brewers is lower, by 40 per cent.,

---

* According to recent European statistics the average longevity of brewers, bakers and butchers is next to the highest among craftsmen (54 years); gardeners and fishermen leading with an average longevity of 58 years.

† Any physician who desires to test the correctness of the tables herein presented, by re-examining any number of men, to be selected by him at random from the entire list, will be assisted by the physicians who made the original examinations, and by the writer of this, in such manner as to facilitate and expedite his undertaking as much as possible.

than the average death-rate among the urban population of the groups of ages corresponding with those to which brewery workmen belong.

III. The health of brewers is unusually good; diseases of the kidneys and liver occur rarely among them.

The conclusion to be drawn from II and III is:

IV. That on an average brewers live longer and preserve their physical energies better than the average workman of the United States.

APPENDIX.

REPORT

OF

MEDICAL EXAMINATIONS

OF

ONE THOUSAND MEN

EMPLOYED IN BREWERIES.

Persons employed in Messrs. H. Clausen & Son Brewing Co., examined by Dr. Guido Katzenmayer.

No.	Initials of Persons Examined.	Age.	Length of Time Employed in Breweries—Years.	Height. Feet—Inches.	Weight—Lbs.	Circumference of Chest—Inches.	Difference in Forced Inspiration and Expiration.	Average Daily Consumption of Malt Beverages, Glasses.	General State of Health.	Condition of Liver.	Condition of Kidneys.	Condition of Heart.	SPECIAL REMARKS.
1	G. M.	44	25	6- 2	215	41	4	20	Good.	Good.	Good.	Good.	
2	T. K.	48	4½	5- 6½	141	36	2	15	"	"	"	"	
3	A. A.	36	16	5- 7	162	36	3	20	"	"	"	"	
4	A. S.	33	7	5- 2	149	36	3	20	"	"	"	"	
5	Ch. H.	23	2½	5-10	210	38	3	40	"	"	"	"	
6	C. H.	46	25	5- 7	225	42	2½	10	"	"	"	"	
7	A. H.	44	10	5- 9	151	36	2	20	"	"	"	"	
8	S. W.	33	16	5- 7¾	163	36	3	30	"	"	"	"	
9	L. H.	44	9	5- 5¾	165	36	2½	25	"	"	"	"	
10	G. Sch.	46	5	5- 8	192	38	3	40	"	"	"	"	
11	W. Sch.	35	5½	5- 9½	153	36	1½	35	Precarious.	"	"	"	On account of hypertrophy of heart.
12	Ch. F.	50	36	5-10¼	186	36	3	50	Good.	"	"	"	
13	G. St.	30	3½	5- 6	165	36	2½	25	"	"	"	"	
14	J. K.	26	5	5- 7¾	160	36	3	50	"	"	"	"	
15	F. K.	27	3	5-	155	35	2½	25	"	"	"	"	
16	J. H.	34	9	5- 9¼	190	38	3	12	"	"	"	"	
17	P. F.	26	9	5- 9½	168	36	3	25	"	"	"	"	
18	F. Sch.	43	9	6- 1	226	40	4	50	"	"	"	"	
19	P. S.	31	1	5- 7¾	152	34	2½	20	"	"	"	"	
20	E. H.	27	3	5- 8½	173	39	4	25	"	"	"	"	
21	J. F.	19	2	5- 9	166	35	3	20	"	"	"	"	
22	F. H.	27	2	5- 8¾	167	36	4	20	"	"	"	"	
23	Th. H.	28	3½	5-10	196	37	3	10	"	"	"	"	
24	J. M.	31	5	5- 7¼	145	35	2	15	"	"	"	"	
25	A. H.	33	4	5- 7½	166	35	3	25	"	"	"	"	
26	W. G.	53	7	5- 1	202	40	3	20	"	"	"	"	
27	Ch. B.	61	22	5- 1	193	38	1½	20	"	"	"	"	
28	G. E.	56	24	5- 7	196	38	2	25	Precarious.	"	"	"	Had symptoms of cirrhosis of liver 1½ years ago.
29	R. P.	35	5	5- 8¾	178	36	2½	10	Good.	"	"	"	
30	Ph. Sch.	38	2	5- 7	179	37	3	50	"	"	"	"	
31	H. D.	26	12	5- 1½	178	36	2¼	25	"	"	"	"	
32	H. B.	38	11	5- 5	144	35	3	5	"	"	"	"	
33	H. A.	39	25	5-10	200	40	2½	20	"	"	"	"	
34	G. G.	43	8	5-11	174	37	2	25	"	"	"	"	
35	S. M.	34	19	5- 6½	204	40	2½	30	"	"	"	"	
36	P. B.	36	6	5- 8	165	38	2¼	5	"	"	"	"	
37	J. H.	33	14	5- 7	167	36	2½	20	"	"	"	"	
38	A. H.	29	12	5- 8	229	40	3	25	"	"	"	"	
39	G. F.	29	7	5- 7	173	35	3	20	"	"	"	"	
40	J. S.	38	18	5- 4	200	40	4	20	"	"	"	"	
41	Ph. F.	34	16	5- 8	187	35	3½	20	"	"	Precarious	"	Had Albuminuria on account of acute congestion of kidneys 1 yr. ago.
42	Ch. D.	21	5	5-10	145	34	2½	12	"	"	Good.	"	
43	Ph. W.	30	2	5-11½	196	38	2½	30	"	"	"	"	
44	G. V.	39	6	5- 6¾	174	39	2¼	20	"	"	"	"	
45	A. S.	34	16	5- 7½	164	35	2½	15	"	"	"	"	
46	F. D.	45	28	5- 7	176	38	3	20	"	"	"	"	
47	F. R.	36	19	5- 5½	175	38	2½	25	"	"	"	"	
48	V. N.	28	6	5-10	153	34	2	30	"	"	"	"	
49	Ch. Sch.	32	12	5- 7	202	40	2	30	"	"	"	"	
50	P. R.	36	10	4- 3	135	33	2	20	"	"	"	"	

Persons employed in Messrs. H. Clausen & Son Brewing Co., examined by Dr. Guido Katzenmayer.—(*Continued.*)

No.	Initials of Persons Examined.	Age.	Length of Time Employed in Breweries—Years.	Height. Feet—Inches.	Weight—Lbs.	Circumference of Chest—Inches.	Difference in Forced Inspiration and Expiration.	Average Daily Consumption of Malt Beverages. Glasses.	General State of Health.	Condition of Liver.	Condition of Kidneys.	Condition of Heart.	SPECIAL REMARKS.
51	J. W.	47	7	5- 6	187	39	4	25	Good.	Good.	Good.	Good.	
52	F. K.	23	11	5- 5	153	36	2¼	5	"	"	"	"	
53	Th. B.	38	10	5- 6½	179	37	2½	10	"	"	"	"	
54	F. S.	51	16	5- 7½	166	37	2½	20	"	"	"	"	
55	K. B.	44	10	5- 8	157	36	2½	20	"	"	"	"	
56	A. S.	26	6	5- 8	168	35	3½	30	"	"	"	"	
57	P. F.	25	¾	5- 9	172	35	2	20	"	"	"	"	
58	Th. S.	29	15	5- 7½	147	35	2½	20	"	"	"	"	
59	A. W.	34	4	5- 8½	151	36	3½	30	"	"	"	"	
60	J. B.	30	4½	5- 5	150	35	2	15	"	"	"	"	
61	J. K.	26	10	5- 4½	135	34	2	6	"	"	"	"	
62	K. Sch.	50	13	5- 8½	242	46	2	5	"	"	"	"	
63	J. U.	28	2	5- 5	145	34	2½	20	"	"	"	"	
64	K. K.	25	4	5- 4	130	32	2	8	"	"	"	"	
65	E. B.	26	5	5- 9½	160	35	3	35	"	"	"	"	
66	F. M.	30	4½	6- 6	177	38	2½	20	"	"	"	"	
67	H. M.	36	8	6- 1	208	37	2	15	"	"	"	"	
68	N. F.	23	10	6- 1	160	34	3	10	"	"	"	"	
69	Ch. K.	20	5	5- 5	174	34	3	6	"	"	"	"	
70	K. G.	30	16	5- 9	219	41	3	10	"	"	"	"	
71	E. E.	33	4	5- 5½	165	35	2½	5	"	"	"	"	
72	W. L.	36	4	5-10	202	34	2½	25	"	"	"	"	
73	S. B.	24	6	5- 8	174	37	3	25	"	"	"	"	
74	J. K.	28	16½	5- 8	147	33	2	25	"	"	"	"	
75	K. K.	28	14	5- 9	223	41	2½	30	"	"	"	"	
76	S. M.	46	15	5- 5	163	37	1½	10	"	"	"	"	
77	G. W.	36	4½	5- 5	148	35	2½	10	"	"	"	"	
78	J. O'N.	20	¾	5- 8	165	36	3	40	"	"	"	"	
79	J. M.	22	2	6- 1	200	40	3	5	"	"	"	"	
80	P. S.	24	4	6- 2	185	40	2	40	"	"	"	"	
81	F. M.	42	10	5- 8	203	39	2½	15	"	"	"	"	
82	L. M.	39	8	5- 5½	161	36	2½	20	"	"	"	"	
83	Ch. M.	38	6	5- 4	135	35	2	20	"	"	"	"	
84	Th. B.	34	9	5- 9	177	38	2½	50	"	"	"	"	
85	M S.	32	5	5- 8	167	35	2½	30	"	"	"	"	
86	I. M.	38	3	5- 8	162	35	2½	12	"	"	"	"	
87	J. Sch.	56	16	5- 7	144	35	2½	20	"	"	"	"	
88	M. A.	39	3	5-11	203	38	2½	20	"	"	"	"	
89	Th. E.	39	12	5- 6	140	36	2	10	"	"	"	"	
90	P H.	29	2½	5- 8	165	35	3	15	"	"	"	"	
91	Ch. H.	39	20	5- 9	163	36	2	30	"	"	"	"	
92	H. F.	47	30	5- 7	210	41	2½	15	"	"	"	"	
93	J. C.	21	7	5-10	183	35	2	15	"	"	"	"	
94	P. B.	36	6	5- 8½	168	38	3	50	"	"	"	"	
95	G. L.	44	10	6- 1	288	45	2½	20	"	"	"	"	
96	H. O.	32	4½	5- 5	197	38	3	10	"	"	"	"	
97	C. Pf.	59	9	5- 9	172	35	2½	5	"	"	"	"	
98	T. H.	28	6	5-10	182	36	2½	5	"	"	"	"	
99	G. D.	23	2	5- 8½	165	35	2	12	"	"	"	"	
100	G. M. M.	44	20	5- 8	213	41	2½	15	"	"	"	"	

Persons employed in Messrs. H. Clausen & Son Brewing Co., examined by Dr. Guido Katzenmayer.—(*Continued.*)

No.	Initials of Persons Examined.	Age.	Length of Time Employed in Breweries—Years.	Height, Feet—Inches.	Weight—Lbs.	Circumference of Chest—Inches.	Difference in Forced Inspiration and Expiration.	Average Daily Consumption of Malt Beverages. Glasses	General State of Health.	Condition of Liver.	Condition of Kidneys.	Condition of Heart.	SPECIAL REMARKS.
101	Ch. P.	38	1½	5- 7	181	38	3	30	Good.	Good.	Good.	Good.	
102	F. E.	38	⅝	5- 8	179	38	2½	15	"	"	"	"	
103	G. G.	29	5	5- 8½	145	35	3	30	"	"	"	"	
104	C. B.	54	26	5-10	189	38	3	50	"	"	"	"	
105	Th. Sch.	33	3	5- 7	193	38	3	40	"	"	"	"	
106	B. Th.	34	3	5- 5	142	35	2½	40	"	"	"	"	
107	H. S.	42	2	5- 6½	170	36	2	40	"	"	"	"	
108	L. K.	34	12	5- 6½	162	35	2½	25	"	"	"	"	
109	M. F.	39	16	5- 6½	177	37	2½	10	"	"	"	"	
110	G. F.	41	8	5- 7	131	34	2	20	"	"	"	"	
111	J. W.	26	5	5- 6	165	37	3	16	"	"	"	"	
112	J. K.	32	15	5-10½	193	38	3	20	"	"	"	"	
113	Ch. E.	29	6	5-10	159	35	2½	20	"	"	"	"	
114	J. Pf.	46	20	5- 5½	148	33	1½	20	Precarious	"	"	"	
115	M. A.	37	9	5- 9	183	38	3	20	Good.	"	"	"	
116	A. McG.	38	10	5- 7½	163	33	2	25	"	"	"	"	
117	B. B.	36	4	5- 7½	172	38	2½	50	"	"	"	"	
118	K. B.	28	5	5-10	159	36	2½	20	"	"	"	"	

Persons employed in Mr. G. Ehret's Brewery, examined by Dr. Guido Katzenmayer.

119	J. B.	28	11	5-11	212	42	3½	25	Good.	Good.	Good.	Good.	
120	A. V.	40	12	5- 8	170	36	2	25	"	"	"	"	
121	G. Z.	36	16	5- 7½	163	35	2½	30	"	"	"	"	
122	G. E. H.	29	1½	5- 9	185	37	2¾	20	"	"	"	"	
123	B. S.	28	12	5-10	206	37	3	30	"	"	"	"	Had Congestion of Kidneys two years ago with Albuminuria.
124	X. K.	43	26	5- 7½	234	47	4	40	"	"	"	"	
125	F. E.	21	1½	5-10	150	35	3	15	"	"	"	"	
126	L. R.	26	2½	5- 5½	176	34	2½	25	"	"	"	"	
127	H. H.	27	2½	5-10½	218	40	4	25	"	"	"	"	
128	K. R.	33	6	5- 7	171	36	3	40	"	"	"	"	
129	K. S.	25	10	5- 7	175	38	3	20	"	"	"	"	
130	J. H.	48	34	5- 8½	188	40	2½	40	"	"	"	"	
131	J. B.	35	5	5- 7½	162	36½	3	20	"	"	"	"	
132	F. B.	21	2½	5- 8½	164	35	3	20	"	"	"	"	
133	J. F.	30	7	5- 8	176	36	2	25	"	"	"	"	
134	L. G.	28	5	5- 6½	150	35	2½	10	"	"	"	"	
135	F. B.	33	17	5- 7	185	40	3	35	"	"	"	"	
136	W. L.	38	11	5- 8	175	35	2½	30	"	"	"	"	
137	I. M.	31	8	5- 7	154	35	2½	25	"	"	"	"	
138	G. B.	25	4	5- 9	162	36	3	40	"	"	"	"	
139	H. R.	20	6	5- 7½	155	35	2½	30	"	"	"	"	
140	E. B.	30	16	5- 4	138	34	2	16	"	"	"	"	
141	J. K.	20	½	5-10	151	35	2½	20	"	"	"	"	
142	W. B.	30	6	5- 4	140	33	2½	40	"	"	"	"	

Persons employed in Mr. G. Ehret's Brewery, examined by Dr. Guido Katzenmayer.—(*Continued.*)

No.	Initials of Persons Examined.	Age.	Length of Time Employed in Breweries—Years.	Height. Feet—Inches.	Weight—Lbs.	Circumference of Chest—Inches.	Difference in Forced Inspiration and Expiration.	Average Daily Consumption of Malt Beverages. Glasses.	General State of Health.	Condition of Liver.	Condition of Kidneys.	Condition of Heart.	SPECIAL REMARKS.
143	Ch. Sch.	37	3	5– 7	165	36	3	30	Good.	Good.	Good.	Good.	
144	F. B.	46	3	5– 6½	165	37	2¾	15	"	"	"	"	
145	R. K.	27	5½	5– 7	170	35	2½	30	"	"	"	"	
146	V. Sp.	26	7	5– 6	158	35	2	25	"	"	"	"	
147	J. K.	36	10	5– 8	173	35	2½	25	"	"	"	"	
148	W. V.	43	8	5– 7	166	34	2	20	"	"	"	"	
149	L. J.	39	7	5– 9½	200	39	4	25	"	"	"	"	
150	G. W.	33	5½	5–11	167	35	3	25	"	"	"	"	
151	B. Eh.	26	10	5– 5	156	35	2½	35	"	"	"	"	
152	P. B.	26	5	5– 8½	159	35	2	30	"	"	"	"	
153	H. L.	31	10	5– 7½	155	36	3	25	"	"	"	"	
154	F. S.	32	9	5– 5	165	37	3	30	"	"	"	"	
155	K. K.	21	7	5– 7	155	35	2½	30	"	"	"	"	
156	Ad. B.	23	10	5–10	170	38	2	25	"	"	"	"	
157	F. H.	30	6	5– 3	157	35	3	40	"	"	"	"	
158	R. Eh.	27	9	4– 5	140	35	2	30	"	"	"	"	
159	Al. Sch.	24	5	5– 8½	179	35	3½	50	"	"	"	"	
160	Wm. St.	28	12	5– 7	155	37	2½	25	"	"	"	"	
161	B. G.	48	13	6–	205	39	4	20	"	"	"	"	
162	K. F.	26	12	5– 8½	187	38	3	50	"	"	"	"	
163	J. Br.	43	26	5– 5	153	36	3	30	"	"	"	"	
164	J. M.	19	½	5–10	165	36	3	30	"	"	"	"	
165	Ph. M.	37	23	5– 7	178	37	3	30	"	"	"	"	
166	A. R.	31	15	5– 6	170	37	3	25	"	"	"	"	
167	J. K.	32	16	5– 6	165	42	3	50	"	"	"	"	
168	J. G.	37	14	5– 6	143	36	2	30	"	"	"	"	
169	J. Gr.	24	8	5– 8	163	36	3	20	"	"	"	"	
170	Wm. G	43	4½	5– 9	215	42	4	30	"	"	"	"	
171	G. R.	27	13	5– 7	186	43	4	50	"	"	"	"	
172	Jo. Alb.	28	10	5– 6½	170	37	3	30	"	"	"	"	
173	Alb. L.	25	3½	5– 8	173	37	3	10	"	"	"	"	
174	A. R.	36	15	6– 3	216	39	2½	50	"	"	"	"	
175	C. M.	36	8	5–10	208	37	3	35	"	"	"	"	
176	Ch. B.	29	3	5– 4	127	33	2	40	"	"	"	"	
177	Jos. S.	30	13	5– 6½	169	37	3	30	"	"	"	"	
178	Alb. W	20	¼	5– 7	148	34	2	10	"	"	"	"	
179	Ch. E.	27	10	5– 6	150	35	2	15	"	"	"	"	
180	Ch. M.	41	5	5– 6½	192	37	3	20	"	"	"	"	
181	L. H.	25	10	5– 7	164	35	2½	20	"	"	"	"	
182	Al. K.	32	16	5– 6½	165	34	2¾	25	"	"	"	"	
183	L. F	39	6	5– 7½	150	34	2	30	"	"	"	"	
184	H. D.	20	6	5– 6½	143	33	2½	20	"	"	"	"	
185	M B.	37	7	5– 6	216	40	3½	30	"	"	"	"	
186	M. G	39	7	5– 9½	205	40	3	35	"	"	"	"	
187	G. Kl.	45	19	5– 9	155	35	3	30	"	"	"	"	
188	P Sp.	44	24	5–10	232	41	3	40	"	"	"	"	
189	R. Er.	24	10	5– 5	156	35	2½	35	"	"	"	"	
190	Wm. St.	42	25	5– 5	148	35	3	20	"	"	"	"	
191	M. B.	29	8	5– 9	128	34	2	30	"	"	"	"	
192	L. L.	42	14	5– 5	170	40	2½	25	"	"	"	"	

Persons employed in Mr. G. EHRET's Brewery, examined by Dr. GUIDO KATZENMAYER.—(*Continued.*)

No.	Initials of Persons Examined	Age.	Length of Time Employed in Breweries—Years.	Height. Feet—Inches.	Weight—Lbs.	Circumference of Chest—Inches.	Difference in Forced Inspiration and Expiration.	Average Daily Consumption of Malt Beverages. Glasses.	General State of Health.	Condition of Liver.	Condition of Kidneys.	Condition of Heart	SPECIAL REMARKS.
193	P. G.	41	20	5-11	263	46	3	20	Good.	Good.	Good.	Good.	
194	G. E.	42	18	5- 7½	226	42	3	20	"	"	"	"	
195	G. B.	35	9	6- 2	214	40	3	30	"	"	"	"	
196	J. St.	24	9	5- 6½	155	33	3	30	"	"	"	"	
197	G. S.	17	1	5- 3	153	35	2	25	"	"	"	"	
198	H. M.	38	15	5- 9½	206	38	1½	25	"	"	"	"	
199	A. W.	20	5	5- 8	175	35	3	25	"	"	"	"	
200	Th. Kl.	33	⅝	6-	228	40	2½	30	"	"	"	"	
201	A. Sch.	26	7	5- 9½	168	35	3	30	"	"	"	"	
202	K. B.	27	3	5- 8½	179	35	4	25	"	"	"	"	
203	J. K.	26	7	5-10	166	36	3	30	"	"	"	"	
204	K. Kl.	40	20	5- 8	180	37	3	25	"	"	"	"	
205	L. Sch.	30	13	5- 7	170	36	2	30	"	"	"	"	
206	A. R.	46	9½	5- 8	173	36	2½	15	"	"	"	"	
207	M. D.	30	15	5- 6	155	36	3	30	"	"	"	"	
208	G. Ga.	26	13	5- 7	203	39	4	40	"	"	"	"	
209	Ph. S.	23	9	5- 6	184	37	3	40	"	"	"	"	
210	A. F.	23	8	5- 7	196	38	2½	60	"	"	"	"	
211	Eb. St.	25	14	5- 6	169	38	2	35	"	"	"	"	
212	Ad. L.	30	1½	5- 4	175	35	2	15	"	"	"	"	
213	W. B.	30	10	5- 7	159	35	2	35	"	"	"	"	
214	E. McD.	48	6	6-	228	42	3	70	"	"	"	"	
215	G. H.	24	3½	5- 7	201	40	3	40	"	"	"	"	
216	F. Sch.	33	22	5- 7	200	40	3½	25	"	"	"	"	
217	J. H.	36	4½	5- 4	214	43	3	20	"	"	"	"	
218	J. M.	31	10	5- 7	212	39	3	20	"	"	"	"	
219	C. P.	28	4	5- 4	179	40	2½	20	"	"	"	"	
220	Ch. E.	31	8	5- 9½	173	35	3	40	"	"	"	"	
221	Fk. W	29	10	5-11½	192	34	3	25	"	"	"	"	
222	F. Sch.	27	8	5-10	186	36	3	25	"	"	"	"	
223	Ch. B.	30	16	5- 8	197	38	3	70	"	"	"	"	
224	A. M.	27	12	5- 9	176	35	3	25	"	"	"	"	
225	G. W.	30	6	5- 9½	166	36	3	50	"	"	"	"	
226	G. S.	54	5½	5- 8½	165	35	2	15	"	"	"	"	
227	F. M.	42	16	5-10	168	36	3	20	"	"	"	"	
228	Ch. R.	28	⅝	5-10	176	35	3	15	"	"	"	"	
229	J. W.	47	22	5- 9½	278	45	3	30	"	"	"	"	Had Abscess of Liver 1½ years ago.
230	Ch. W.	31	18	5- 1	145	36	2	10	"	"	"	"	
231	J. M.	27	12	5- 8	140	35	3	10	"	"	"	"	
232	B. E.	37	6	5- 5	141	35	3	10	"	"	"	"	
233	G. D.	35	8	5- 9	208	40	3	20	"	"	"	"	
234	J. W.	27	5	5- 7	165	35	2½	30	"	"	"	"	
235	J. St.	37	9	6-	186	38	3	15	"	"	"	"	
236	B. Eg.	54	31	5- 6	159	37	3	40	"	"	"	"	
237	F. St.	30	21	5- 6	168	38	3	45	"	"	"	"	
238	D. H.	25	2½	5- 7	175	35	2½	20	"	"	"	"	
239	G. Sch.	22	2	5- 2½	144	34½	2½	40	"	"	"	"	
240	A. O.	43	8	5- 9½	175	35	2½	30	"	"	"	"	
241	J. B.	52	11	5- 8	190	40	3	30	"	"	"	"	
242	K. G.	20	2	5- 6½	147	34	3	40	"	"	"	"	

Persons employed in Mr. G. Ehret's Brewery, examined by Dr. Guido Katzenmayer.—(*Continued.*)

No.	Initials of Persons Examined.	Age.	Length of Time Employed in Breweries—Years.	Height. Feet—Inches.	Weight—Lbs.	Circumference of Chest—Inches.	Difference in Forced Inspiration and Expiration.	Average Daily Consumption of Malt Beverages. Glasses.	General State of Health.	Condition of Liver.	Condition of Kidneys.	Condition of Heart	SPECIAL REMARKS.
243	F. W.	28	⅜	5– 7½	162	35	2¼	35	Good.	Good.	Good.	Good.	
244	J. Kl.	39	2½	5– 2½	149	36	2½	20	"	"	"	"	
245	St. K.	27	10m	5– 9	138	35	2½	30	"	"	"	"	
246	G. M.	40	16	5– 8	170	36	3	20	"	"	"	"	
247	F. D.	57	12	5– 4	160	37	2½	15	"	"	"	"	
248	G. H.	42	12	5– 9	149	34	2½	10	"	"	"	"	
249	K. L.	26	½	4– 5	154	35	3	20	"	"	"	"	
250	A. M.	27	2	5– 3½	148	36	2½	30	"	"	"	"	
251	A. G.	42	1½	5–10½	163	37	2½	15	"	"	"	"	
252	M. Sch.	24	1½	5– 6½	180	36	3	30	"	"	"	"	
253	H. B.	24	1½	5– 9	186	36	4	30	"	"	"	"	
254	K. R.	35	10	5– 8	170	36	2½	25	"	"	"	"	
255	G. E.	27	8	5– 4	152	32	1½	10	Precarious	"	"	"	On account of tuberculous infiltration of lungs.
256	G. H.	35	10	5– 8	170	38	3	25	Good.	"	"	"	
257	J. Sch.	46	1½	5–10	219	40	3	30	"	"	"	"	
258	J. D.	37	2	5– 5	146	32	2	10	"	"	"	"	
259	J. W.	33	2	5– 5½	142	34	2	30	"	"	"	"	
260	P. S.	43	12	5– 8½	224	42	4	25	"	"	"	"	
261	J. L.	34	4	5– 8	180	37	2	20	"	"	"	"	
262	O. A.	60	4	5–6½	145	34	2½	15	"	"	"	"	
263	Th. B.	23	½	5– 5	145	33	2½	10	"	"	"	"	
264	R. B.	36	11	5–10½	181	36	3	15	"	"	"	"	
265	J. K.	31	10	5– 7½	166	35	2½	40	"	"	"	"	
266	P. M.	36	1½	5– 8	166	35	3	25	"	"	"	"	
267	P. C.	58	10	5–10½	217	44	2½	20	"	"	"	"	
268	S. B.	24	½	5– 6	156	35	2½	20	"	"	"	"	
269	A. M.	25	5	5– 7	165	34½	2½	30	"	"	"	"	
270	A. A.	26	5	5– 7	218	36	2½	20	"	"	"	"	
271	H. M.	32	7	5– 6	134	33	2½	15	"	"	"	"	
272	P. Z.	34	3	5– 2½	185	40	3	30	"	"	"	"	
273	P. Sch.	43	1½	5– 7½	202	38	3	10	"	"	"	"	
274	T. V	30	4	5– 9	154	34	2½	25	"	"	"	"	
275	H. F.	27	5	5– 8	161	36	2	30	"	"	"	"	
276	H. W.	21	1	5– 6	136	32	2	7	"	"	"	"	
277	P. B.	28	5	5– 9½	163	35	2½	40	"	"	"	"	
278	P. M.	25	½	5– 4	140	33	1½	20	"	"	"	"	
279	J. P. S.	43	6	5– 6	179	35	2½	10	"	"	"	"	
280	A. McD.	18	⅜	5– 8	141	34	2	15	"	"	"	"	
281	R. H	48	3	5– 6	135	32	2	5	"	"	"	"	
282	H K.	54	9	5– 7½	160	35	2	20	"	"	"	"	
283	J. M.	38	1½	5– 7½	157	35½	1½	15	"	"	"	"	
284	M. St.	37	21	5– 9	196	39	2½	25	"	"	"	"	
285	E. L.	39	22	5– 6½	168	38	2	20	"	"	"	"	
286	G. B.	26	7	5– 9½	191	38	2	20	"	"	"	"	
287	L. G.	35	16	5– 9	173	38	2	20	"	"	"	"	
288	A. W.	34	¾	5–10	193	36	2½	20	"	"	"	"	
289	J. B.	21	5	5– 8	177	37	2	40	"	"	"	"	
290	R. R.	22	1	5– 6	147	33	2	10	"	"	"	"	
291	L. H.	36	20	5– 3½	154	35	2½	30	"	"	"	"	
292	S. St.	30	4	5– 9	170	35	2½	25	"	"	"	"	

Persons employed in Mr. G. EHRET'S Brewery, examined by Dr. GUIDO KATZENMAYER.—(*Continued.*)

No.	Initials of Persons Examined.	Age.	Length of Time Employed in Breweries—Years.	Height, Feet—Inches.	Weight—Lbs.	Circumference of Chest—Inches.	Difference in Forced Inspiration and Expiration.	Average Daily Consumption of Malt Beverages, Glasses.	General State of Health.	Condition of Liver.	Condition of Kidneys.	Condition of Heart.	SPECIAL REMARKS.
293	P. M.	24	5	5– 9	159	34	3	35	Good.	Good.	Good.	Good.	
294	O. H.	18	½	5– 5	133	32	2½	20	"	"	"	"	
295	M. G.	41	4	5–10	178	35	2½	30	"	"	"	"	
296	J. K.	31	10	5– 8	169	35	2	20	"	"	"	"	
297	Th. C.	28	9	5– 6	157	34	2	12	"	"	"	"	
298	T. McC.	44	8	5– 5½	162	35½	2	15	"	"	"	"	
299	L. Alb.	26	3	5– 6	168	33	3	20	"	"	"	"	
300	J. F.	32	5	5– 5	147	32	2	15	"	"	"	"	

Persons employed in Mr. JACOB RUPPERT'S Brewery, examined by Dr. GUIDO KATZENMAYER.

No.	Initials of Persons Examined.	Age.	Length of Time Employed in Breweries—Years.	Height, Feet—Inches.	Weight—Lbs.	Circumference of Chest—Inches.	Difference in Forced Inspiration and Expiration.	Average Daily Consumption of Malt Beverages, Glasses.	General State of Health.	Condition of Liver.	Condition of Kidneys.	Condition of Heart.	SPECIAL REMARKS.
301	J. R.	19	2	5– 7½	143	33	3	10	Good.	Good.	Good.	Good.	
302	Chs. R.	23	4	5– 7	188	37	2½	10	"	"	"	"	
303	G. E.	35	18	5– 4½	180	40	2½	20	"	"	"	"	
304	H. M.	38	15	5– 4½	187	36	4	20	"	"	"	"	
305	M. G.	43	29	5– 9	186	36	4½	40	"	"	"	"	
306	F. K.	29	13	5–10	184	38	3	25	"	"	"	"	
307	W. H.	29	1	5– 9½	176	36	3	20	"	"	"	"	
308	Fl. M.	35	21	5– 6	177	38	2	35	"	"	"	"	
309	J. J.	34	17	5– 9½	215	41	3	40	"	"	"	"	
310	J. B.	29	6	5– 6	173	36	2	40	"	"	"	"	
311	G. K.	35	16	5– 4	205	40	3	40	"	Precarious	"	"	Had congestion of liver three years ago.
312	H. S.	34	20	5– 6	176	38	3	25	"	Good.	"	"	
313	St. K.	30	16	5– 6½	173	36	3	40	"	"	"	"	
314	J. Sch.	27	10	6– 2½	210	40	3	50	"	"	"	"	
315	J. B.	30	11	6– ½	187	38	4	30	"	"	"	"	
316	J. G.	23	6	5– 9½	160	36	3	30	"	"	"	"	
317	J. D.	41	25	5–10	219	39	3½	40	"	"	"	"	
318	G. R.	25	8	5– 6½	163	36	3	25	"	"	"	"	
319	H. Y.	27	6	5– 6	168	35	2	10	"	"	"	"	
320	R. M.	26	11	5– 5½	150	35	2½	25	"	"	"	"	
321	M. F.	27	5	5– 8½	183	35	2½	30	"	"	"	"	
322	P. Sch.	27	3	5– 6½	154	35	2	20	"	"	"	"	
323	P. A.	30	5	5– 9	183	38	3	15	"	"	"	"	
324	F. K.	25	2	5– 8½	175	37	2	30	"	"	"	"	
325	J. D.	41	24	5– 9½	191	36	3½	50	"	"	"	"	
326	H. G.	36	14	4– 6	170	35	2½	25	"	"	"	"	
327	F. H.	44	16	5– 8½	170	36	2	30	"	"	"	"	
328	G. Sch.	41	20	5– 5	223	40	2½	25	"	"	"	"	
329	J. L.	28	16	6–	163	35	4	50	"	"	"	"	
330	M. E.	41	21	5– 9½	215	39	2½	30	"	"	"	"	
331	A. G.	28	¾	5– 6½	156	35	2½	30	"	"	"	"	
332	J. H.	33	17	5– 6	136	35	2½	20	"	"	"	"	
333	J. F.	28	11	5– 7½	165	38	2	25	"	"	"	"	

Persons employed in Mr. Jacob Ruppert's Brewery, examined by Dr. Guido Katzenmayer.—(*Continued.*)

No.	Initials of Persons Examined.	Age.	Length of Time Employed in Breweries—Years.	Height, Feet—Inches.	Weight—Lbs.	Circumference of Chest—Inches.	Difference in Forced Inspiration and Expiration.	Average Daily Consumption of Malt Beverages. Glasses.	General State of Health.	Condition of Liver.	Condition of Kidneys.	Condition of Heart.	SPECIAL REMARKS.
334	V. O.	36	14	5- 8½	209	42	2½	15	Good.	Good.	Good.	Good.	
335	L. R.	31	5	5- 9½	187	35	2½	10	"	"	"	"	
336	E. L.	44	12	5- 9	167	34	1½	25	"	"	"	"	
337	Ch. St.	34	20	5- 9½	180	37	2½	25	"	"	"	"	
338	Ch. O.	58	10	6-	220	41	2	5	"	"	"	"	
339	F. K.	25	12	5- 7½	149	35	1½	40	"	"	"	"	
340	J. R.	30	14	5- 3½	157	37	3	50	"	"	"	"	
341	H. G.	29	15	5- 8	180	36	3	25	"	"	"	"	
342	C. P.	25	11	6- 1	191	36	4	30	"	"	"	"	
343	J. Sch.	22	2	5- 8	151	35	2½	25	"	"	"	"	
344	W. L.	43	19	5- 7½	171	39	2	15	"	"	"	"	
345	A. M.	26	2½	5- 8	248	41	2½	40	"	"	"	"	
346	J. K.	65	17	5- 8	208	38	2½	15	"	"	"	"	
347	J. K.	20	5	5- 7	152	36	2	20	"	"	"	"	
348	G. K.	24	6	5- 5	162	35	2	25	"	"	"	"	
349	J. W.	30	9	5- 8	175	35	2	25	"	"	"	"	
350	F. K.	22	6	5- 8	174	35	2½	50	"	"	"	"	
351	K. B.	34	14	5- 8	182	42	2	15	"	"	"	"	
352	J. K.	39	14	5- 8	192	38	2½	25	Precarious	"	"	"	Had Endocarditis, caused by acute articular Rheumatism in 1886.
353	Th. N.	30	1½	5- 6½	156	35	3	10	Good.	"	"	"	
354	F. St.	20	1½	5- 7½	155	35	2½	25	"	"	"	"	
355	P. B.	30	10	5-11	183	36	3	20	"	"	"	"	
356	J. D.	30	4	4- 5	148	35	2½	20	"	"	"	"	
357	A. T.	32	6	5- 2½	146	35	2	35	"	"	"	"	
358	J. W	54	7	5- 3	146	34	2	25	"	"	"	"	
359	G. K.	19	½	5- 5½	152	35	2½	20	"	"	"	"	
360	C. D.	33	12	5- 6½	185	38	3	25	"	"	"	"	
361	J. W.	29	8	5-11	188	38	3	15	"	"	"	"	
362	M. H.	31	19	5- 7	163	36	3	40	"	"	"	"	
363	J E.	41	4½	5-11	214	39	3	40	"	"	"	"	
364	K. B.	43	6	5- 4	159	35	2	40	"	"	"	"	
365	K. N.	31	14	5- 8	166	36	3	25	"	"	"	"	
366	A. Pf.	27	14	5- 7	159	35	2	30	"	"	"	"	
367	R. L.	29	2	5- 3½	135	34	2	15	"	"	"	"	
368	A. Sch.	26	2	5- 8	164	35	2	25	"	"	"	"	
369	Ch. V.	49	20	5- 7½	181	38	2	25	"	"	"	"	
370	J. O.	46	16	5- 6½	150	36	2	25	"	"	"	"	
371	F. R.	16	¼	5- 7	161	33	2	6	"	"	"	"	
372	W. K.	22	2	5- 4	151	34½	3	15	"	"	"	"	
373	F. R.	22	1	5-11½	207	38	5	15	"	"	"	"	
374	Ch. Kl.	24	3	6- 1½	186	42	3	20	"	"	"	"	
375	J. M.	37	5½	5- 7½	216	41	3	30	"	"	"	"	
376	K. D	22	4	5-11	178	35	2	5	"	"	"	"	
377	F. M.	31	6½	5- 7	141	34	2½	20	"	"	"	"	
378	J. G. R.	18	1	5- 7½	182	34	3	10	"	"	"	"	
379	A. T.	23	5	5-10	182	35	2½	25	"	"	"	"	
380	G. H.	35	3½	5- 5	162	35	2	10	"	"	"	"	
381	M. N.	38	14	5-10	216	41	3	25	"	"	"	"	
382	W. B.	33	3	5- 6	147	36	1½	20	"	"	"	"	
383	J. M.	29	13	5- 7½	191	38	3	40	"	"	"	"	

Persons employed in Mr. JACOB RUPPERT's Brewery, examined by Dr. GUIDO KATZENMAYER.—(*Continued*)

Persons Examined.	Age.	Length of Time Employed in Breweries—Years.	Height. Feet—Inches.	Weight—Lbs.	Circumference of Chest—Inches.	Difference in Forced Inspiration and Expiration.	Average Daily Consumption of Malt Beverages. Glasses.	General State of Health.	Condition of Liver.	Condition of Kidneys.	Condition of Heart.	SPECIAL REMARKS.
W	35	4	5- 5	171	35	2	50	Good.	Good.	Good.	Good.	
G.	31	7	5-11	178	36	3½	25	"	"	"	"	
G.	23	7	5- 5½	143	34	2	20	"	"	"	"	
E.	25	1½	5- 8	160	35	2	25	"	"	"	"	
W.	32	6	5- 6½	186	36	3	40	"	"	"	"	
R.	31	5	5- 9½	195	39	2½	15	"	"	"	"	
B.	36	16	6- 2½	239	40	3	20	"	"	"	"	
B.	30	3	5- 7	177	35	3	12	"	"	"	"	
Ph.	36	10	5- 7	151	35	2½	30	"	"	"	"	
H.	34	11	5- 8½	222	41	3	10	"	"	"	"	
Z.	37	5	5- 6½	164	37	2	30	"	"	"	"	
S.	24	6	5- 8½	169	34	3	15	"	"	"	"	
H.	36	22	5-10	168	36	2½	20	"	"	"	"	
R.	24	9	5- 9	186	37	2½	35	"	"	"	"	
M.	42	28	5- 5	159	36	2½	30	"	"	"	"	
L.	34	20	6-	213	39	4	25	"	"	"	"	
O.	35	20	5- 3½	182	37	2½	20	"	"	"	"	
ch.	40	24	5- 8	175	36	3½	15	"	"	"	"	
G.	41	22	6-11	200	38	3½	30	"	"	"	"	
N.	30	4	5-11	211	40	3	50	"	"	"	"	
H.	25	11	5- 4½	140	34	3	15	"	"	"	"	
S.	37	13	5- 8	180	36	3	25	"	"	"	"	
H.	37	18	5- 5½	210	41	2½	12	"	"	"	"	
E.	27	4½	5-10	165	36	2½	25	"	"	"	"	
St.	20	½	5-10	174	35	3	10	"	"	"	"	
B.	35	19	5- 7	176	41	2	30	"	"	"	"	
G.	45	20	5-10	171	36	3	25	"	"	"	"	
S.	31	15	5- 8½	171	35	2½	20	"	"	"	"	
K.	35	10	5-10½	176	34	2	15	"	"	"	"	
M.	29	3	5- 8	220	40	2½	40	"	"	"	"	
N.	19	½	5- 7½	149	33	3	15	"	"	"	"	
B.	40	20	5- 8	175	36	3	30	"	"	"	"	Had acute Hepatitis last year.
ch.	35	5½	5- 9	163	37	3	30	"	"	"	"	
R.	33	16	5-10	175	35	3	25	"	"	"	"	
cA.	55	3	5- 5	163	35	2	10	"	"	"	"	
K.	52	9	5- 6	188	38	3	50	"	"	"	"	
ch.	23	7	5- 7	170	37	2½	20	"	"	"	"	
K.	25	½	5- 5	147	33	2½	25	"	"	"	"	
A.	29	1¼	5- 8	135	33	2½	10	"	"	"	"	
B.	33	20	6- 1	212	38	2½	20	"	"	"	"	
J.	40	7	5- 4	181	38	3	25	"	"	"	"	
T.	38	9	5- 6½	173	36	1½	20	"	"	"	"	
H.	59	5	5-11½	184	36	2½	10	"	"	"	"	
J.	40	25	5- 8½	194	37	3	40	"	"	"	"	
V.	28	7	5- 6	158	35	3	30	"	"	"	"	
Pf.	31	17	5- 8½	188	37	4	30	"	"	"	"	
S.	28	8	5- 6½	147	33	3	30	"	"	"	"	
J.	30	2½	5- 6	170	36	4	20	"	"	"	"	
St.	37	20	5- 5	190	38	2½	50	"	"	"	"	
B.	23	9	5-11	172	36	3	20	"	"	"	"	

Persons employed in Mr. Jacob Ruppert's Brewery, examined by Dr. Guido Katzenmayer.—(*Continued.*)

No	Initials of Persons Examined	Age	Length of Time Employed in Breweries—Years	Height Feet—Inches	Weight—Lbs	Circumference of Chest—Inches	Difference in Forced Inspiration and Expiration	Average Daily Consumption of Malt Beverages, Glasses	General State of Health	Condition of Liver	Condition of Kidneys	Condition of Heart	SPECIAL REMARKS
434	J. Sch.	27	6	5- 8½	168	35	2	40	Good.	Good.	Good.	Good.	
435	J. E.	23	4	5- 4½	154	35½	2	20	"	"	"	"	
436	Fr. W.	32	11	5- 5	162	36	2½	25	"	"	"	"	
437	Ch. H.	42	28	5- 5½	177	36	2½	15	"	"	"	"	
438	J. K.	48	11	5-10½	207	39	4½	20	"	"	"	"	
439	K. Sch.	24	7	5-11	184	35½	3½	20	"	"	"	"	
440	V. B.	30	10	5- 7½	162	35	2½	25	"	"	"	"	
441	J. H.	32	6	5- 3	141	35	2½	30	"	"	"	"	
442	A. G.	42	25	5-10½	198	38	2½	60	"	"	"	"	
443	Gtf. T.	31	16	5- 8	178	37	4	50	"	"	Precarious.	"	Had acute Congestion of Kidneys 1½ years ago.
444	G. L.	44	25	5-10½	170	34½	2½	25	"	"	Good.	"	
445	Ch. F.	41	12	5- 7½	176	34½	2½	25	"	"	"	"	
446	Ed. El.	33	17	5- 8	195	37	5	25	"	"	"	"	
447	K. R.	23	6	5- 7	156	34	2	30	"	"	"	"	
448	G. B.	37	14	5- 5	168	36	2	10	"	"	"	"	
449	J. M.	44	5	5- 8	169	35½	2½	20	"	"	"	"	
450	Chs. R.	25	½	5- 9	167	34	2	15	"	"	"	"	
451	R. M.	30	5	5- 7½	178	38	4	30	"	"	"	"	
452	G. H.	37	4½	5- 7½	151	34½	2½	15	"	"	"	"	

Persons employed in Messrs. G. Ringler & Co.'s Brewery, examined by Dr. Guido Katzenmayer.

No	Initials of Persons Examined	Age	Length of Time Employed in Breweries—Years	Height Feet—Inches	Weight—Lbs	Circumference of Chest—Inches	Difference in Forced Inspiration and Expiration	Average Daily Consumption of Malt Beverages, Glasses	General State of Health	Condition of Liver	Condition of Kidneys	Condition of Heart	SPECIAL REMARKS
453	O. D.	36	21	5- 8½	224	44	2½	20	Good.	Good.	Good.	Good.	
454	J. St.	26	4½	5- 8½	187	37	3	12	"	"	"	"	
455	F. B.	19	3	5-10½	178	35	3	25	"	"	"	"	
456	L. J.	34	5	5- 4½	163	35	2½	18	"	"	"	"	
457	F. H.	34	13	5- 5½	172	37	2½	25	"	"	"	"	
458	B. V.	38	10	5- 9½	162	36	2½	25	"	"	"	"	
459	J. J.	22	9	5- 7	153	35	2	20	"	"	"	"	
460	G. R.	35	6	5-11	186	37	2	25	"	"	"	"	
461	G. H.	31	5	5-10	191	38	3	25	"	"	"	"	
462	J. H.	36	19	6- 1	195	38	3	30	"	"	"	"	
463	A. H.	35	18	5- 6½	193	39	3	25	"	"	"	"	
464	W. K.	25	8	5- 6½	165	35	3	25	"	"	"	"	
465	Ch. H.	40	12	5- 4½	146	35	1½	25	"	"	"	"	
466	A. H.	38	18	5- 8½	204	40	2	25	"	"	"	"	
467	K. W.	40	20	5- 8½	154	35	2½	25	"	"	"	"	
468	V. Sch.	34	16	5- 8½	161	36	3	20	"	"	"	"	
469	L. Z.	33	4	6- 2	239	41	2½	25	"	"	"	"	
470	A. V.	39	21	5- 4	147	35	2	20	"	"	"	"	
471	J. B.	35	6	5- 8½	207	42	2	25	"	"	"	"	
472	A. F.	33	15	5- 4	155	34	2½	35	"	"	"	"	
473	J. Sch.	38	22	5- 5	168	36	2½	20	"	"	"	"	
474	Ch. W.	29	11	5- 4	149	33	3	30	"	"	"	"	
475	H. K.	28	11	5- 7½	186	38	3	30	"	"	"	"	

Persons employed in Messrs G. RINGLER & Co.'s Brewery, examined by Dr. GUIDO KATZENMAYER (*Continued.*)

Initials of Persons Examined.	Age.	Length of Time Employed in Breweries—Years.	Height. Feet—Inches.	Weight—Lbs.	Circumference of Chest—Inches.	Difference in Forced Inspiration and Expiration.	Average Daily Consumption of Malt Beverages. Glasses.	General State of Health.	Condition of Liver.	Condition of Kidneys.	Condition of Heart.	SPECIAL REMARKS.
J. M.	29	½	5- 4	146	34	2½	20	Good.	Good.	Good.	Good.	
F. Pf.	23	½	5- 8	172	35	3	15	"	"	"	"	
F. K.	48	20	5- 6½	180	36	2	10	"	"	"	"	
K. N.	32	9	5- 7½	182	36	2½	15	"	"	"	"	
J. S.	39	4	5- 6½	179	38	2½	25	"	"	"	"	
M. M.	28	18	5- 8	159	35	2½	20	"	"	"	"	
B. Hitz	36	10	5- 9	231	40	2½	40	"	"	"	"	
Ch. R.	51	39	5-10	258	43	3	40	"	"	"	"	
J. G.	51	40	5- 8	198	38	3	20	"	"	"	"	
G. D.	37	21	5- 6½	153	35	2	20	"	"	"	"	
P. S.	39	25	5- 8	165	37	2½	20	"	"	"	"	
J. N.	41	7	5- 8	178	36	2½	20	"	"	"	"	
F. Kl.	22	3	5-10	179	37	2½	25	"	"	"	"	
A. K.	27	5	5- 7½	155	35	2½	20	"	"	"	"	
J. N.	33	10	5- 7	155	35	2½	20	"	"	"	"	
K. J.	33	1½	5- 6	174	37	2½	15	"	"	"	"	
F. Z.	42	16	5- 3½	169	36	2½	25	"	"	"	"	
J. A.	40	13	5-10½	182	35	2½	40	"	"	"	"	
A. B.	24	5	5-11	213	39	3	20	"	"	"	"	
J. H.	33	10	5- 7½	187	37	2½	15	"	"	"	"	
J. R.	24	15	5- 9½	162	34	2½	30	"	"	"	"	
J. Sch.	20	8	5- 7	180	36	2	15	"	"	"	"	
W. F.	31	7	5- 9½	180	38	3	20	"	"	"	"	
A. H.	28	1½	6- 1	221	39	3	8	"	"	"	"	
M. G.	28	9	5- 9½	180	37	3	35	"	"	"	"	
K. St.	34	6	5- 7	194	39	3	35	"	"	"	"	
F. K.	36	8	5- 8	182	37	2½	25	"	"	"	"	
H. Z.	45	12	5-11½	163	37	2	20	"	"	"	"	
Ch. W.	63	16	5- 7	171	36	2½	12	"	"	"	"	
F. K.	27	2	5- 9½	163	35	2½	30	"	"	"	"	
E. Z.	44	9	5-10	176	36	2½	30	"	"	"	"	
O. H.	19	¾	5- 6½	146	33	2	18	"	"	"	"	
M. A.	36	4½	5- 5	172	36	2	20	"	"	"	"	
J. K.	26	2½	5- 5½	171	36	3	25	"	"	"	"	
Fr. H.	24	10	5- 6½	180	39	2½	30	"	"	"	"	
W. B.	36	15	5- 8½	181	36	3	30	"	"	"	"	
W. L. D	33	1½	5- 6	144	31	2	10	"	"	"	"	
A. K.	35	19	5-10½	176	38	1½	40	"	"	"	"	
X. W	40	23	5- 5	159	37	2	30	"	"	"	"	
H. St.	45	20	5- 9	203	37	3	10	Precarious Good.	"	"	"	Had Endocarditis, caused by acute articular Rheumatism in 1880.
F. K.	34	½	6- 2	181	37	3	20		"	"	"	
J. G.	37	19	4- 5	150	34	2½	10	"	"	"	"	
J. T.	26	3	5- 3½	142	35	2	20	"	"	"	"	
K. D.	44	2½	5- 3	147	36	2	25	"	"	"	"	
Ch. F.	37	19	5- 8½	167	36	3	20	"	"	"	"	
J. W.	27	3½	5- 6½	168	36	3	20	"	"	"	"	
F. G. S.	22	1	5- 8	157	34	2	10	"	"	"	"	
W. R.	19	2	5- 5	137	33	2	12	"	"	"	"	
F. M. F.	45	30	5- 8	169	37	3	30	"	"	"	"	
F. K.	29	8	5- 8½	189	36	2½	25	"	"	"	"	

Persons employed in Messrs. G. RINGLER **&** Co.'s Brewery, examined by **Dr. Guido** KATZENMAYER.—(*Continued.*)

No.	Initials of Persons Examined.	Age.	Length of Time Employed in Breweries—Years.	Height, Feet—Inches.	Weight—Lbs.	Circumference of Chest—Inches.	Difference in Forced Inspiration and Expiration.	Average Daily Consumption of Malt Beverages. Glasses.	General State of Health.	Condition of Liver.	Condition of Kidneys.	Condition of Heart.	SPECIAL REMARKS.
526	C. R.	45	6	5- 9	182	36	2½	10	Good.	Good.	Good.	Good.	
527	J. Sch.	32	10	5- 7½	192	37	2	20	"	"	"	"	
528	M. W.	28	7	5- 5¾	162	35	2	15	"	"	"	"	
529	K. T.	32	8	5- 6½	159	35	2¼	20	"	"	"	"	
530	K. A.	36	3½	6- 1½	189	37	2½	15	"	"	"	"	
531	J. H.	49	5	6- 2	169	36	2	20	"	"	"	"	
532	Ch. H.	38	5	5- 8	185	37	2½	20	"	"	"	"	
533	A. B.	28	6	5- 6½	172	38	2½	25	"	"	"	"	
534	F. Sch.	40	8	5- 7	184	37	2½	15	"	"	"	"	
535	Ch. J.	32	7	5- 5½	160	36	2½	25	"	"	"	"	

Persons employed in **Messrs. F.** & M. SCHAEFER Brewing Co., examined by **Dr.** GUIDO KATZENMAYER.

No.	Initials of Persons Examined.	Age.	Length of Time Employed in Breweries—Years.	Height, Feet—Inches.	Weight—Lbs.	Circumference of Chest—Inches.	Difference in Forced Inspiration and Expiration.	Average Daily Consumption of Malt Beverages. Glasses.	General State of Health.	Condition of Liver.	Condition of Kidneys.	Condition of Heart.	SPECIAL REMARKS.
536	J. B.	37	24	5- 7½	200	39½	3¾	6	Good.	Good.	Good.	Good.	
537	J. D.	34	6	5-10¾	245	39	4	12	"	"	"	"	
538	F. L.	52	7	5- 8	138	34	2	8	"	"	"	"	
539	E. S.	37	1	5- 7	165	36	2½	15	"	"	"	"	
540	G. M.	30	½	5- 6	160	35	2½	20	"	"	"	"	
541	M. M.	35	20	5-10½	218	39	3	30	"	"	"	"	
542	J. R.	20	1	5- 8¾	186	37	3	25	"	"	"	"	
543	V. B.	46	25	5- 7	250	44½	2½	10	"	"	"	"	
544	J. B.	28	12	5-10	198	36	5	30	"	"	"	"	
545	J. W.	25	10	5- 7	173	35	3	30	"	"	"	"	
546	J. K.	42	20	5- 9	177	36	4	30	"	"	"	"	
547	K. T.	27	11	5- 7	175	34	3½	30	"	"	"	"	
548	Fz. T.	45	14	5- 8	188	39	3½	30	"	"	"	"	
549	J. W.	28	12	5- 6½	155	33	3	35	"	"	"	"	
550	W. E.	30	8	5- 8	150	35	3	40	"	"	"	"	
551	Ch. W.	32	9	5- 5	163	36	2½	25	"	"	"	"	
552	W. B.	27	10	5- 9½	203	38	3	20	"	"	"	"	
553	F. K.	36	20	5- 5	150	33	2	25	"	"	"	"	
554	F. Sch.	26	8	5- 8½	180	37	2½	40	"	"	"	"	
555	O. Sch.	27	12	5- 5	180	38½	2½	40	"	"	"	"	
556	Ch. K.	43	15	5-10½	185	37	4	25	"	"	"	"	
557	L. M.	32	20	5- 5½	175	36	2½	25	"	"	"	"	
558	H. B.	19	½	5- 8½	175	34	2½	30	"	"	"	"	
559	A. Kl.	26	12	5- 7½	185	35	2½	30	"	"	"	"	
560	H. D.	38	20	5-10½	204	38½	3½	25	"	"	"	"	
561	M. Sch.	39	15	5- 7½	195	37	3	25	"	"	"	"	Had Icterus two years ago.
562	J. R.	29	9	5- 7½	190	38	4	30	"	"	"	"	
563	H. Sch.	34	6	5- 6½	162	34	2	20	"	"	"	"	
564	W. O.	25	10	5- 7	208	39	3	35	"	"	"	"	
565	A. F.	37	22	5- 9	187	39	4½	30	"	"	"	"	
566	J. F.	45	7	5- 2	134	33	1½	20	"	"	"	"	

Persons employed in Messrs. F. & M. Schaefer Brewing Co., examined by Dr. Guido Katzenmayer.—(*Continued.*)

No.	Initials of Persons Examined.	Age.	Length of Time Employed in Breweries—Years.	Height, Feet—Inches.	Weight—Lbs.	Circumference of Chest—Inches.	Difference in Forced Inspiration and Expiration.	Average Daily Consumption of Malt Beverages. Glasses.	General State of Health.	Condition of Liver.	Condition of Kidneys.	Condition of Heart.	SPECIAL REMARKS.
567	F. K.	28	6	5- 8	185	37	4	20	Good.	Good.	Good.	Good.	
568	Th. B.	36	6	5- 5	140	33	2½	20	"	"	"	"	
569	Th. L.	26	1½	5- 7½	170	35	2½	20	"	"	"	"	
570	A. S.	26	1½	5- 8½	170	35½	2½	20	"	"	"	"	
571	J. K.	45	15	5- 7¾	175	36	2½	25	"	"	"	"	
572	W. M.	35	2½	5- 6½	156	35	3	15	"	"	"	"	
573	J. K.	41	8½	5-10½	200	39	4	15	"	"	"	"	
574	R. K.	25	2	5-8¾	168	36½	3	20	"	"	"	"	
575	Fz. Sch.	37	23	5-10	210	39	3½	20	"	"	"	"	
576	P. N.	36	20	5- 5	180	37	4	20	"	"	"	"	
577	F. N.	32	13	5- 8½	155	34	1½	25	"	"	"	"	
578	Fk. Pf.	26	7	5- 8¾	180	36½	2½	25	"	"	"	"	
579	E. Sch.	30	14	5- 5½	172	36½	2	20	"	"	"	"	
580	J. D.	32	3½	5- 2	135	31	2	20	"	"	"	"	
581	F. M.	28	5	5- 8¾	185	34	4	20	"	"	"	"	
582	Ch. K.	51	5	5- 5	160	35	3	20	"	"	"	"	
583	A. E.	28	4	5-10	195	37	4	25	"	"	"	"	
584	W. B.	23	4	5- 9½	168	36	3	30	"	"	"	"	
585	H. B.	34	15	6- ½	186	35	3	25	"	"	"	"	
586	H. H.	33	6	5- 8	204	37	3	25	"	"	"	"	
587	J. B.	41	6½	5- 6½	230	42	2½	20	"	"	"	"	
588	Gv. T.	20	5	5-11¾	163	34	4	15	"	"	"	"	
589	A. St.	23	10	5- 4	165	35	2	8	"	"	"	"	
590	J. W.	39	5	5- 6½	170	36	3	20	"	"	"	"	
591	A. D.	27	4	5- 8	200	38	4½	20	"	"	Precarious	"	Had acute Congestion of Kidneys with Albuminuria 2½ years ago.
592	F. D.	23	8	5-11¾	178	35	3½	20	"	"	Good.	"	
593	K. F.	31	7	5-11	190	36	4	25	"	"	"	"	
594	A. Sch.	43	25	5-11¾	195	37	2½	20	"	"	"	"	
595	A. E.	28	16	5- 4¾	165	35	2½	20	"	"	"	"	
596	A. Sch.	36	2	5- 3¾	173	36	2	15	"	"	"	"	
597	V. H.	45	9	5- 4½	152	35	2½	20	"	"	"	"	
598	J. Sch.	48	14	5- 6	162	35	3	20	"	"	"	"	
599	J. R.	30	7	5-11	185	34	2½	35	"	"	"	"	
600	J. F.	37	4	5- 7½	189	36	2½	20	"	"	"	"	
601	H. E.	43	6	5- 6¾	165	37	3	20	"	"	"	"	
602	W. V.	37	17	5- 9	270	43	3½	25	"	"	"	"	
603	G. Ch.	54	11	5- 7	163	37½	1½	35	"	"	"	"	
604	Fz. B.	28	8	5-10½	175	36	3	30	"	"	"	"	
605	J. D.	42	19	5- 7	190	37½	3	15	"	"	"	"	
606	Ch. B.	39	24	5- 8	163	34	2½	20	"	"	"	"	
607	J. S.	44	14	5- 4¾	137	34	1½	15	"	"	"	"	
608	Chs. N.	25	11	5- 9	179	35	3	50	"	"	"	"	

Persons employed in Mr. Fr. Oppermann's (Jr.) Brewery, examined by Dr. Guido Katzenmayer.

609	C. P.	30	6	5-11	192	39	2½	30	Good.	Good.	Good.	Good.	
610	Ch. G.	42	5	5-10½	184	37	2½	25	"	"	"	"	

Persons employed in Mr. Fr. Oppermann's (Jr.) Brewery, examined by Dr. Guido Katzenmayer.—(*Continued.*)

No.	Initials of Persons Examined.	Age.	Length of Time Employed in Breweries—Years.	Height, Feet—Inches.	Weight—Lbs.	Circumference of Chest—Inches.	Difference in Forced Inspiration and Expiration.	Average Daily Consumption of Malt Beverages, Glasses.	General State of Health.	Condition of Liver.	Condition of Kidneys.	Condition of Heart.	Special Remarks.
611	J. M.	18	2	5- 5½	123	30	3½	7	Good.	Good.	Good.	Good.	
612	J. H.	35	11	5- 8	252	44	3	50	"	"	"	"	
613	M. L.	53	40	5- 6	198	41	2	7	"	"	"	"	
614	M. St.	33	16	5-10	256	45	2½	25	"	"	"	"	
615	R. L.	39	15	5- 7	155	37	2½	15	"	"	"	"	
616	H. K.	21	2	5- 9	166	36	3½	25	"	"	"	"	
617	M. R.	25	7	5- 7	157	35	2	30	"	"	"	"	
618	P. Ch.	26	13	5- 8½	176	37	2½	40	"	"	"	"	
619	G. D.	28	12	5- 5¾	157	38	2	20	"	"	"	"	
620	J. J.	21	10	5- 8	154	36	3	40	"	"	"	"	
621	G. J.	29	17	5- 5½	142	33	2	20	"	"	"	"	
622	H. B.	33	12	5- 8	185	39	3	20	"	"	"	"	
623	K. L.	28	4	5- 8	172	38	2	25	"	"	"	"	
624	G. B.	30	12	5- 9½	178	38	2½	30	"	"	"	"	
625	E. K.	33	5	5- 6¼	158	36	2	40	"	"	"	"	
626	J. N.	49	17	5- 7	175	36	1½	25	"	"	"	"	
627	W. M.	41	7	6- 1	230	43	2	15	"	"	"	"	
628	M. M.	19	4	5- 4½	120	32	2	10	"	"	"	"	
629	W. R.	29	3	5-10	165	35	2½	20	"	"	"	"	
630	Th. F.	39	12	5- 6	205	38½	4	15	"	"	"	"	
631	J. D.	49	3	5- 7	186	41	3	20	"	"	"	"	
632	R. C.	24	8	5- 5¾	162	34	3	15	"	"	"	"	
633	J. B.	32	16	5- 8	179	38	3	15	"	"	"	"	
634	J. D.	35	5	5- 8¾	168	35	2½	35	"	"	"	"	
635	J. Z.	28	13	5- 7½	168	36	2	50	"	"	"	"	
636	A. R.	32	7	5- 7½	253	43	3	50	"	"	"	"	
637	A. O.	33	4	5-11½	186	37	3	15	"	"	"	"	
638	G. W.	30	15	5- 8½	190	39	2½	40	"	"	"	"	
639	A. Sch.	50	30	5- 9½	168	36	2	45	"	"	"	"	
640	P. S.	30	13	5- 6	166	35	3	30	"	"	"	"	
641	A. H.	29	7	5-11½	270	44	2	40	"	"	"	"	
642	W. A.	34	8	5- 5½	165	36	2½	25	"	"	"	"	
643	J. K.	39	23	5- 7	190	39	3	20	"	"	"	"	
644	L. M.	26	5	5- 9	170	36	2½	25	"	"	"	"	
645	C. K.	38	6	5- 8½	173	38	2½	15	"	"	"	"	
646	A. Sch.	31	18	5- 2	140	35	2	15	"	"	"	"	
647	J. R.	34	16	5- 6½	195	39	3	20	"	"	"	"	
648	H. E.	40	20	5- 4½	143	35	2½	20	"	"	"	"	
649	D. Sch.	30	7	5- 9	165	38	2	50	"	"	"	"	
650	Fr. Fr.	40	25	5- 7½	163	37	2	30	"	"	"	"	
651	Ch. S.	26	14	5- 8	176	37	3	50	"	"	"	"	
652	A. M	26	7	5- 8½	155	34	2½	50	"	"	"	"	
653	P. W.	25	12	5- 9	184	37	4	50	"	"	"	"	
654	J. B.	29	12	5- 9½	182	38	2	40	"	"	"	"	
655	C. P.	31	5	5- 5	140	35½	3	12	"	"	"	"	
656	J. O.	25	13	5- 5½	225	40	3½	25	"	"	"	"	
657	G. Z.	42	21	5- 9	175	37	2	20	"	"	"	"	
658	K. R.	33	19	5- 6½	152	36	2½	15	"	"	"	"	
659	M. L.	41	7	5- 9	165	35	2½	20	"	"	"	"	
660	J. D.	17	2	5- 3	105	30	1½	5	"	"	"	"	

Persons employed in Mr. J. Chr. Hüpfel's Brewery, examined by Dr. Guido Katzenmayer.

No.	Initials of Persons Examined.	Age.	Length of Time Employed in Breweries—Years.	Height, Feet—Inches.	Weight—Lbs.	Circumference of Chest—Inches.	Difference in Forced Inspiration and Expiration.	Average Daily Consumption of Malt Beverages, Glasses.	General State of Health.	Condition of Liver.	Condition of Kidneys.	Condition of Heart.	SPECIAL REMARKS.
661	G. M.	41	25	5- 5¾	187	37½	2	15	Good.	Good.	Good.	Good.	
662	Ph. H.	30	4	5- 5½	135	32½	3	10	"	"	"	"	
663	F. B.	36	2½	5- 6½	152	34	2	15	"	"	"	"	
664	W. K.	30	7	5-10	283	46	3	40	"	"	"	"	
665	F. K.	39	20	5- 9½	194	37	4	35	"	"	"	"	
666	L. W.	29	15	5- 8	157	34	3	40	"	"	"	"	
667	P. L.	30	9	5- 7½	219	39	5	30	"	"	"	"	
668	B. Sch.	38	23	5- 5½	155	35½	3½	25	"	"	"	"	
669	A. E.	29	15	5-10	200	37	4	35	"	"	"	"	
670	K. H.	28	4½	5- 8	165	36	3	20	"	"	"	"	
671	J. M.	34	20	5- 9	175	38½	3½	50	"	"	"	"	
672	J. St.	26	6	5- 5	151	35	2½	20	"	"	"	"	
673	D. B.	19	½	5- 8	158	34	3	20	"	"	"	"	
674	F. T.	25	7	5- 5	148	35	2½	40	"	"	"	"	
675	J. B.	33	2	5- 7½	163	38	4½	35	"	"	"	"	
676	A. U.	41	7	5- 3½	155	36	2½	15	"	"	"	"	
677	M. M.	35	1½	5- 8	170	36	3½	25	"	"	"	"	
678	G. G.	43	6	5- 9	168	36½	2	20	"	"	"	"	
679	W. Sp.	30	2½	5- 7	160	34	3½	30	"	"	"	"	
680	F. M.	19	5	5- 9	165	34	1½	15	"	"	"	"	
681	W. A.	25	8	5- 6	145	34	2	20	"	"	"	"	
682	V. N.	23	5	5- 7½	164	36	3	25	"	"	"	"	
683	S. M.	47	20	5- 9½	171	36	3	20	"	"	Precarious	"	Had acute Congestion of Kidneys two years ago with Albuminuria.
684	C. E.	44	1	5- 6½	154	35	2½	15	"	"	Good.	"	
685	F. L.	27	5	5- 9	170	35½	3	20	"	"	"	"	
686	K. R.	34	18	5-11¾	172	36	4	25	"	"	"	"	
687	J. W.	32	10	5- 3½	153	36	3	20	"	"	"	"	
688	J. G.	42	8	5- 9¾	225	41	2	20	"	"	"	"	
689	A. D.	56	40	5- 4	179	38	2	15	"	"	"	"	
690	M. Sch.	27	10	5- 5	162	35	2½	30	"	"	"	"	
691	W. B.	24	7	5- 8	180	36	2½	15	"	"	"	"	

Persons employed in Messrs. J. Kress Brewing Co., examined by Dr. Guido Katzenmayer.

692	H. G.	47	30	5-10	219	41	3	10	Good.	Good	Good.	Good	
693	F. F.	26	11	5-11	294	45	4	30	"	"	"	"	
694	U. R.	45	26	5- 7½	267	45	2½	20	"	"	"	"	
695	A. B.	34	18	5- 3	160	37	1½	25	"	"	"	"	
696	G. A.	37	17	5-10	211	40	2½	15	"	"	"	"	
697	W. R.	57	5	5- 6	159	35	2	10	"	"	"	"	
698	F. M.	25	5	5- 6	170	37	4	15	"	"	"	"	
699	G. L.	28	13	5- 7	188	39	3	30	"	"	"	"	
700	J. B.	32	2	5- 6	162	37	4	20	"	"	"	"	
701	G. C.	35	16	5- 9	206	37	2½	15	"	"	"	"	
702	J. B.	33	6	5- 8½	213	41	3	15	"	"	"	"	

Persons employed in Messrs. J. Kress Brewing Co., examined by Dr Guido Katzenmayer.—(*Continued.*)

No.	Initials of Persons Examined.	Age.	Length of Time Employed in Breweries—Years.	Height. Feet—Inches.	Weight—Lbs.	Circumference of Chest—Inches.	Difference in Forced Inspiration and Expiration.	Average Daily Consumption of Malt Beverages. Glasses.	General State of Health.	Condition of Liver.	Condition of Kidneys.	Condition of Heart.	SPECIAL REMARKS.
703	G. St.	65	3	5- 4½	162	36	2	12	Good.	Good.	Good.	Good.	
704	G. E.	22	4	5- 5½	145	34	2½	20	"	"	"	"	
705	A. E.	26	8	5-10	166	34	2½	5	"	"	"	"	
706	A. St.	43	7	5- 7	170	35	2½	20	"	"	"	"	
707	J. H.	42	10	5- 8	155	34	3	25	"	"	"	"	
708	J. S.	39	17	5- 3	205	40	3½	25	"	"	"	"	
709	J. M.	45	4	5- 4	119	33	2	5	"	"	"	"	
710	W. Sch.	25	3	5-10½	157	36	2½	20	"	"	"	"	
711	J. Sch.	39	17	5- 4	157	36	2½	30	"	"	"	"	
712	Ch. B.	38	1	5- 4½	145	35	2	20	"	"	"	"	
713	A. St.	40	10	5- 5	180	37	2½	30	"	"	"	"	
714	J. Sch.	45	23	5- 7	199	40	3	10	"	"	"	"	
715	G. G.	30	14	5- 7½	172	36	2½	30	"	"	"	"	
716	V. S.	29	14	5-10½	180	38	2½	25	"	"	"	"	
717	G. O.	38	16	5- 7½	210	38	3	20	"	"	"	"	
718	J. G.	39	20	5- 6½	165	35	1½	20	"	"	"	"	
719	K. R.	47	25	5- 4½	159	37	3½	40	"	"	"	"	
720	H. G. jr.	20	3	5- 6½	165	35	2	25	"	"	"	"	
721	J. N.	22	2	5- 5½	155	35	3	20	"	"	"	"	
722	J. M.	32	14	5- 7	170	36	3	20	"	"	"	"	
723	J. H.	32	17	5- 5½	185	38	4½	40	"	"	"	"	
724	W. M.	55	22	5- 6	151	36	2½	30	"	"	"	"	
725	J. D.	40	8	5- 4	140	34	1½	20	"	"	"	"	
726	Chs. W.	45	4	5- 6	153	36	1½	20	"	"	"	"	
727	J. W.	21	9	5- 8	168	35	2	5	"	"	"	"	
728	F. L.	24	2½	5- 4½	136	34	2	10	"	"	"	"	
729	J R.	43	13	5- 6½	156	36	2½	25	Precarious	"	"	"	Had acute Hepatitis three years ago.
730	J. W	20	2	5- 8½	171	34	2	10	Good.	"	"	"	
731	J. H.	38	1	5- 8½	176	34	3½	15	"	"	"	"	
732	A. N.	20	1	5- 6½	155	35	2½	20	"	"	"	"	
733	J. P.	43	9	5- 7½	154	35	2	10	"	"	"	"	
734	J. H.	25	2	5- 7	170	35	3½	25	"	"	"	"	
735	G. B.	40	10	5- 6½	151	35	3	20	"	"	"	"	
736	J. W.	39	23	6-	250	42	3½	40	"	"	"	"	

Persons employed in **Messrs. G.** Winter & Co.'s Brewery, examined by Dr. Guido Katzenmayer.

737	F. N.	33	16	5-11	195	39	4	20	Good.	Good.	Good.	Good.	
738	F. St.	39	6	5- 6½	158	37	2½	25	"	"	"	"	
739	J. St.	36	10	5-11½	176	35	2½	60	"	"	"	"	
740	G. V	38	20	5-11	212	41	2½	50	"	"	"	"	
741	M. Gr	26	5	5- 8	179	37	2½	20	"	"	"	"	
742	Ch. H	23	6	5- 5	158	36	3	20	"	"	"	"	
743	J N	33	5	5- 7½	175	37	2½	20	"	"	"	"	
744	J. Fl.	45	30	5- 6½	170	39	2½	30	"	"	"	"	

Persons employed in Messrs. G. WINTER & Co.'s **Brewery, examined by** Dr. GUIDO KATZENMAYER—(*Continued.*)

No.	Initials of Persons Examined.	Age.	Length of Time Employed in Breweries—Years.	Height, Feet—Inches.	Weight—Lbs.	Circumference of Chest—Inches.	Difference in Forced Inspiration and Expiration.	Average Daily Consumption of Malt Beverages, Glasses.	General State of Health	Condition of Liver.	Condition of Kidneys.	Condition of Heart.	SPECIAL REMARKS.
745	H. Sch.	34	17	5— 3	155	36	4	25	Good.	Good.	Good.	Good.	
746	J. H.	27	5	5— 6	170	34	3	20	"	"	"	"	
747	J. W.	40	24	5— 7½	170	38	2½	25	"	"	"	"	
748	J. B.	30	6	5— 8½	200	40	4	20	"	"	"	"	
749	J. B.	39	7½	5— 6	180	38	3	30	"	"	"	"	
750	O. O.	35	9	5— 6½	158	36	3½	20	"	"	"	"	
751	Ch. Gl.	33	6	5— 5½	155	34	2½	20	"	"	"	"	
752	W. St.	38	15	5— 8½	159	36	2½	30	"	"	"	"	
753	A. Sch.	30	15	5— 6	160	35	3	40	"	"	"	"	
754	A. K.	24	½	5— 9	169	37	2½	20	"	"	"	"	
755	J. N.	30	7	5— 5½	185	39	2½	20	"	"	"	"	
756	A. K.	34	15	6— 3½	289	41	4	30	"	"	"	"	
757	Fz. M.	35	20	5— 3	170	34	3	30	"	"	"	"	
758	K. G.	27	9	5— 5	157	35	4	20	"	"	"	"	
759	F. H.	41	13	5— 3½	215	39	3	30	"	"	"	"	
760	A. R.	50	10½	5— 7	163	37	3	25	"	"	"	"	
761	Ch. E.	39	12	5— 8½	180	42	2½	30	"	"	"	"	
762	B. N.	42	5	5— 5½	170	40	3	30	"	"	"	"	
763	Chs. H.	42	6	5— 9	176	37	2½	30	"	"	"	"	
764	H. N.	33	10	5— 5	158	36½	2½	30	"	"	"	"	
765	A. St.	34	13	5— 6½	175	38	3	30	"	"	"	"	
766	D. M.	32	6	5— 8	168	35	2	25	"	"	"	"	
767	K. Sch.	50	9	5— 6½	175	38	2½	25	"	"	"	"	

Persons employed in Mr. JACOB HOFFMANN's Brewery, **examined by** Dr. GUIDO KATZENMAYER.

No.	Initials of Persons Examined.	Age.	Length of Time Employed in Breweries—Years.	Height, Feet—Inches.	Weight—Lbs.	Circumference of Chest—Inches.	Difference in Forced Inspiration and Expiration.	Average Daily Consumption of Malt Beverages, Glasses.	General State of Health	Condition of Liver.	Condition of Kidneys.	Condition of Heart.	SPECIAL REMARKS.
768	Hy. H.	22	6	5— 7	180	36	3	15	Good.	Good.	Good.	Good.	
769	A. B.	30	7	5— 8	188	38	2½	25	"	"	"	"	
770	J. R.	34	5	5— 7	168	35	3½	8	"	"	"	"	
771	R. M.	45	27	5— 7	175	35	3	30	"	"	"	"	
772	J. M.	42	12	6—	205	39	3	40	"	"	"	"	
773	P. Sch.	25	5	5—11½	198	36	5	20	"	"	"	"	
774	O. L.	30	15	5— 5	160	35	2	60	"	"	"	"	
775	H. L.	34	17	5— 7	190	39	4½	40	"	"	"	"	
776	Th. D.	43	10	5— 9	200	36	4	15	"	"	"	"	
777	J. V.	46	14	5— 9	230	37	4	20	"	"	"	"	
778	P. O.	37	8	5— 7	154	35	2½	15	"	"	"	"	
779	A. W.	46	8	5— 6½	183	37	3	35	"	"	"	"	
780	G. H.	43	6	5—10	170	35	3	20	"	"	"	"	
781	Ch. W.	25	5	5—11	183	38	2½	15	"	"	"	"	
782	H. G.	44	11	5— 9	175	35	2½	10	Precarious	Precarious	"	"	Suffered from Icterus twice within the past three years.
783	F. S.	40	20	5— 5	160	35½	2½	40	Good.	**Good.**	"	"	
784	F. R.	37	4	5— 7	168	35	3	30	"	"	"	"	
785	W. Sch.	50	5	5— 8½	184	39	4	15	"	"	"	"	
786	J. R.	24	4	5— 5½	158	34½	3	20	"	"	"	"	

Persons employed in Mr. Jacob Hoffmann's Brewery, examined by Dr. Guido Katzenmayer—(*Continued.*)

No.	Initials of Persons Examined.	Age.	Length of Time Employed in Breweries—Years.	Height. Feet—Inches.	Weight—Lbs.	Circumference of Chest—Inches.	Difference in Forced Inspiration and Expiration.	Average Daily Consumption of Malt Beverages. Glasses.	General State of Health.	Condition of Liver.	Condition of Kidneys.	Condition of Heart.	SPECIAL REMARKS.
787	J. B.	38	10	5- 8	183	38	2½	20	Good.	Good.	Good.	Good.	
788	W. St.	27	2½	5- 9½	210	39	3	20	"	"	"	"	
789	Th. H.	32	5	5- 9	195	38	5	30	"	"	"	"	
790	A. H.	34	3	5- 7	150	33	2½	15	"	"	"	"	
791	G. H.	26	10	5- 7	185	39	4	60	"	"	"	"	
792	J. H.	44	28	5-10	170	38	2½	50	"	"	"	"	
793	J. S.	33	9	5- 5	165	34	2½	15	"	"	"	"	
794	M. K.	37	4	5- 5	145	34	1½	15	"	"	"	"	
795	F. K.	30	1½	5-10	170	34½	3½	20	"	"	"	"	
796	K. M.	37	15	5- 6	152	35	2	30	"	"	"	"	
797	J. W.	27	10	5- 1	130	34	2½	25	"	"	"	"	
798	K. B.	43	½	5- 9	165	38	3	12	"	"	"	"	
799	L. K.	25	11	5-10	172	37	3	20	"	"	"	"	
800	A. J.	18	2m	5-10	165	34	2½	15	"	"	"	"	
801	P. K.	34	10	5- 8	162	35	2½	50	"	"	"	"	
802	J. Sch.	44	1½	5- 6	175	37	3	15	"	"	"	"	
803	Ph. G.	23	5	5- 7	190	36	2½	15	"	"	"	"	

Persons employed in Fink & Son's Brewery, examined by Dr. H. F. Kudlich.

No.	Initials of Persons Examined.	Age.	Length of Time Employed in Breweries—Years.	Height. Feet—Inches.	Weight—Lbs.	Circumference of Chest—Inches.	Difference in Forced Inspiration and Expiration.	Average Daily Consumption of Malt Beverages. Glasses.	General State of Health.	Condition of Liver.	Condition of Kidneys.	Condition of Heart.	SPECIAL REMARKS.
804	A. M.	51	31	5- 5½	187	39½	2	20	Good.	Normal.	Normal.	Normal.	
805	W. Z.	21½	4	5- 4	162	33	1¾	20	"	"	"	"	Gained over 30 lbs. since he has been working in brewery.
806	W. H.	46	30	5- 5½	186	37½	3	25	"	"	"	"	
807	J. R.	29	6	5- 6½	207	39	2½	25	"	"	"	"	
808	J. G. L.	29	15	5-11½	184	37	2½	25	"	"	"	"	
809	A. E.	32	8	5- 9½	184	36½	2½	15	"	"	"	"	
810	A. J.	43	6	5- 8¾	168	35¾	2	20	"	"	"	"	
811	T. B.	41	10	5- 8	150	33½	1¾	15	"	"	"	"	
812	O. S.	39	20	5- 8	187	38	2½	30	"	"	"	"	
813	J. D.	32	5½	5- 6½	172	35½	3	35	"	"	"	"	
814	A. K.	24	10	5-10	165	36½	3½	25	"	"	"	"	
815	J. M.	30	16	5- 6½	166	37	2¾	25	"	"	"	"	
816	J. L.	23	7	5- 3½	133	32½	2½	15	"	"	"	"	
817	H. V.	24	5½	5- 6	162	38¾	1	25	Not good.	Good.	Good.	Good.	Suffers from emphysema.
818	L. Z.	39	21	5- 9	164	37	3	30	Good.	"	"	"	
819	W. A.	26	15	5- 7¼	185	35	2½	15	"	"	"	"	
820	O. R.	32	15	5- 6	161	35½	2½	20	"	"	"	"	

Persons employed in Burr, Son & Co.'s Brewery, examined by Dr. H. F. Kudlich.

No.	Initials of Persons Examined	Age.	Length of Time Employed in Breweries—Years.	Height, Feet—Inches.	Weight—Lbs.	Circumference of Chest—Inches.	Difference in Forced Inspiration and Expiration.	Average Daily Consumption of Malt Beverages. Glasses.	General State of Health.	Condition of Liver.	Condition of Kidneys.	Condition of Heart.	SPECIAL REMARKS.
821	W. M.	42	15	5– 8¼	185	39	3	20	Good.	Good.	Good.	Good.	Never been sick.
822	J. B.	45	30	5– 7¼	190	37	2	20	"	Normal.	Normal.	Normal.	
823	A. B.	36	19	5–10	238	44	3	15	Robust.	"	"	"	Never been sick.
824	K. W.	30	12	5– 9	212	38	2	20	Good.	"	"	"	
825	L. K.	25	10	5– 5½	192	38	2½	25	"	"	"	"	
826	L. M.	27	8	5– 6¾	174	34¾	1½	10	"	"	"	"	
827	A. Z.	30	14	5– 8¼	198	38	2	20	"	"	"	"	
828	G. M.	36	23	5– 8	195	38	2½	25	"	"	"	"	
829	G. W.	18½	1¾	5– 6	140	34½	3	10	"	"	"	"	
830	H. O.	42	22	5– 8	247	46	1	20	"	Enlarged.	Good.	Good.	Rheumatism.
831	A. B.	38	7	5– 6½	185	38½	1½	15	"	Good.	"	"	
832	A. K.	31	18	5– 9¼	186	37	2½	25	"	"	"	"	
833	J. S.	32	17	5– 6	166	38	2½	15	"	"	"	"	
834	H. H.	31	15	5– 8¼	160	33¼	3	20	"	"	"	"	
835	J. W.	32	06	5– 7½	185	36¼	2	15	"	"	"	"	
836	E. F.	63	38	5– 5	161	37	1¾	20	"	"	"	"	
837	G. W.	56	32	5– 8¾	250	54	2	30	Robust.	"	"	"	Never been sick.
838	A. S.	27	9	5– 9	172	34	3¼	15	"	"	"	"	
839	T. M.	47	20	5– 8½	172	37	2	20	Good.	Normal.	Normal.	Normal.	
840	K. K.	38	20	5– 4	212	41	2	25	Robust.	"	"	"	Never been sick
841	A. W.	27	1½	5– 8	170	33	3	15	Good.	"	"	"	
842	C. K.	45	25	5– 6½	180	36	1½	15	Weak.	"	"	"	Suf'rs frequently from Bronchitis.
843	F. K.	28	14	5– 9½	180	37	2½	20	Good.	"	"	"	
844	L. O.	16	4	5– 6	143	33	2	5	"	"	"	"	
845	A. W.	54	28	5– 8	185	38¼	2½	15	"	"	"	"	
846	M. M.	26	5	5– 7	153	35¼	1½	25	"	"	"	"	
847	E. M.	28	10	5– 7½	174	36¾	2½	15	"	"	"	"	
848	P. McC	48	15	5– 8	185	37½	2½	10	"	"	"	"	
849	J. S.	54	20	5– 6	145	34	1½	..	Not good.	"	"	Diseased.	Suffers from Rheumatism.

Persons employed in Beadleston & Woerz' Brewery, examined by Dr. H. F. Kudlich.

850	F. R.	36	8¼	5– 8½	146	37	1¾	10	Good.	Normal.	Normal.	Normal.	
851	F. T.	45	16	5– 7	173	39	2	8	Not good.	"	"	Diseased.	Suf'rs frequently from Rheumatism.
852	J. L.	38	9	5– 9	212	40	2¼	20	Good.	"	"	Normal.	
853	E. R.	28	13	5– 7½	165	36½	2½	10	Robust.	"	"	"	
854	H. G.	34	5	5– 5	149	35	2	12	Good.	"	"	"	
855	C. M.	40	8	5– 7¼	190	38½	2½	14	"	"	"	"	
856	P. B.	19	7	5– 8	159	36	2	15	"	"	"	"	
857	O. D.	33	13	6–	220	41½	2¾	15	Very good	"	"	"	Never been sick.
858	W. N.	24	6	5–11	181	33	3	25	Good.	"	"	"	
859	H. G.	34	6	5– 7½	176	38	2	20	"	"	"	"	
860	J. K.	25	6	5–11	244	42	2½	20	Robust.	"	"	"	Never been sick.
861	M. E.	34	2	5– 7½	173	38½	2	15	Good.	"	"	"	
862	J. S.	32	4	5– 5½	160	35	1½	20	"	"	"	"	

Persons employed in Beadleston & Woerz' **Brewery,** examined by **Dr. H. F.** Kudlich.—(*Continued.*)

No.	Initials of Persons Examined.	Age.	Length of Time Employed in Breweries—Years.	Height, Feet—Inches.	Weight—Lbs.	Circumference of Chest—Inches.	Difference in Forced Inspiration and Expiration.	Average Daily Consumption of Malt Beverages. Glasses.	General State of Health.	Condition of Liver.	Condition of Kidneys.	Condition of Heart.	SPECIAL REMARKS.
863	H. H.	37	2	5- 6½	165	37½	2	10	Good.	Normal.	Normal.	Normal.	
864	A. H.	38	5½	5- 9	168	38	3	20	"	"	"	"	
865	L. O.	48	9	5- 8	182	36	2	15	"	"	"	"	
866	O. G.	31	2½	5- 8½	169	34	2½	20	"	"	"	"	
867	A. N.	30	12	5- 7½	184	37½	2½	15	"	"	"	"	
868	J. S.	48	12	5- 4	136	32	1½	18	Weak.	"	"	"	Suffers fr'm chr. Bronchitis.
869	J. J.	29	10	5- 8½	213	38½	2	25	Robust.	"	"	"	
870	J. C.	37	3	5- 8½	178	35½	2½	30	Good.	"	"	"	
871	H. S.	26	2	5- 9½	200	38	3	20	Robust.	"	"	"	
872	F. E.	29	10m	5- 4	137	32½	3	15	Good.	"	"	"	
873	H. K.	25	9 "	5- 7½	175	36	3	10	"	"	"	"	
874	J. A.	30	2½	5- 7½	169	34	3½	15	"	"	"	"	
875	Z. S.	43	4½	5- 8	204	40	2	20	"	Enlarged.	"	"	
876	W. S.	27	1	5- 5	150	33½	2	18	"	Normal.	"	"	
877	P. B.	21	2	5- 8½	176	36	2½	10	"	"	"	"	
878	M. F.	38	7	5- 9	190	37	2½	10	"	"	"	"	
879	K. P.	27	4	5- 9½	158	33½	2	15	"	"	"	"	
880	F. M.	36	5½	5- 7½	163	35½	2½	10	"	"	"	"	
881	S. W.	61	24	6-	185	36	2½	24	"	"	"	"	Never been sick.
882	P. K.	29	5	5- 7	214	38½	2½	15	Robust.	"	"	"	Never been sick.
883	F. F.	43	7½	5- 6	174	36	1½	25	Good.	"	"	"	
884	J. S.	34	8	5-10	200	38	2	24	"	"	"	"	
885	E. H.	33	6½	5- 6	135	32	3	6	"	"	"	"	
886	M. F.	26	4	5-10	200	38	2¾	15	Robust.	"	"	"	
887	J. S.	50	15	6- 2	187	37	2½	12	"	"	"	"	Never been sick.
888	P. **S.**	30	16	5- 8	175	36	1¾	10	Good.	"	"	"	
889	Z. **B.**	28	14	5- 7	195	38	2	10	"	"	"	"	
890	S. **L.**	49	10	5- 4¾	134	33½	1½	12	"	"	"	"	
891	G. **W.**	37	8	5- 5	175	35	2½	20	"	"	"	"	
892	C. **D.**	27	9m	5- 6	160	35	1¾	18	"	"	"	"	
893	W. **L.**	31	5½	5- 8	165	35½	1¾	15	"	"	"	"	
894	D. **C.**	35	7	5- 8	165	35	1½	18	"	"	"	"	
895	**J. S.**	45	8	5- 9½	178	38	2	7	"	"	"	"	
896	H. F.	30	10m	5-11	200	38	3	16	**Robust.**	"	"	"	
897	F. H. K.	25	10m	5- 9	172	36	1¾	10	**Good.**	"	"	"	
898	K. S	23	6	5-10½	207	36½	2½	20	**Robust.**	"	"	"	
899	P. D.	26	1	5- 7	157	32	2½	15	**Good.**	"	"	"	
900	**G. S.**	32	9m	5- 9	178	38	2½	16	"	"	"	"	
901	**N. B.**	35	10	5-10	187	37	3	15	"	"	"	"	
902	**B. M.**	36	4½	5- 5	182	35½	2	10	"	"	"	"	
903	H. **F. K.**	42	5	5- 9	220	40	2¾	15	**Robust.**	"	"	"	
904	**O. D.**	20	8	5- 7	161	33	2	20	**Good.**	"	"	"	
905	B. **H.**	37	25	5- 6½	183	37½	1¾	30	"	"	"	"	
906	E. T.	32	9	5- 8½	175	38	2	40	"	"	"	"	
907	A. O.	27	9	5- 5½	141	32	1½	25	"	"	"	"	
908	P. L.	29	2½	6-	207	39½	2½	30	Robust.	"	"	"	
909	G. V. **D.**	38	**12**	5-10½	190	38½	2	10	Good.	"	"	"	
910	M. H.	23	**5**	5- 9	196	39	3	20	Robust.	"	"	"	
911	H. B.	39	**13**	5- 6½	170	37½	**2**	15	Good.	"	"	"	
912	J. B.	**24**	**5**	5- 6	204	38½	**2½**	15	"	"	"	"	

Persons employed in BEADLESTON & WOERZ' Brewery, examined by Dr. H. F. KUDLICH (*Continued.*)

No.	Initials of Persons Examined.	Age.	Length of Time Employed in Breweries—Years.	Height. Feet—Inches.	Weight—Lbs.	Circumference of Chest—Inches.	Difference in Forced Inspiration and Expiration.	Average Daily Consumption of Malt Beverages. Glasses.	General State of Health.	Condition of Liver.	Condition of Kidneys.	Condition of Heart.	SPECIAL REMARKS.
913	L. S.	36	15	5–10	204	40½	2¾	30	Robust.	Normal.	Normal.	Normal.	
914	C. R.	25	11	5– 4	165	35	2½	12	Very good	“	“	“	
915	F. W.	35	17	5– 7	175	36	2	30	Good.	“	“	“	
916	E. L.	26	1	5– 9	178	39¼	2	25	“	“	“	“	
917	E. B.	20	4	5– 7	158	34¾	1¾	20	“	“	“	“	
918	J. K.	28	12	6–	200	38¼	2¼	25	“	“	“	“	
919	A. R.	38	4	5– 7	174	36	2	25	“	“	“	“	
920	K. S.	26	8	5– 6¾	280	33	2	25	“	“	“	“	
921	A. H.	32	17	5– 6½	178	35	2½	75	“	“	“	“	
922	K. S.	35	20	5– 5¾	209	39½	2	25	“	“	“	“	
923	A. H.	27	8	5– 5	148	32¾	1½	15	“	“	“	“	
924	J. B.	24	10	5– 7	180	36	2	25	“	“	“	“	
925	J. T.	36	22	5– 9	195	38½	2	10	“	“	“	“	
926	A. H.	25	14	5– 9	209	37¾	2	30	Robust.	“	“	“	
927	G. A.	24	3	5– 8½	185	37	2	20	Good.	“	“	“	
928	C. S.	37	12	5– 8	209	40½	2	10	Not good.	“	“	Diseased.	Suffers from Rheumatism.
929	H. S.	37	5	5– 9	172	37	2½	20	Good.	“	“	Normal.	
930	J. M.	44	24	5–11	209	39	2	25	Not good.	Enlarged.	“	“	
931	G. R.	37	9	5– 7½	171	37	2	20	Good.	Normal.	“	“	

Persons employed in S. LIEBMANN SONS' Brewery, examined by Dr. HUGO KOETHE, 57 Montrose Ave., Brooklyn, E. D.

932	J. B.	31	5½	67½	182	39	39–41½	20	Good.	Normal.	Normal.	Normal.	
933	J. K.	46	15	63	152	37	37–39½	24	“	“	“	“	
934	G. S.	39	9	67	156	34	34–36	30	“	“	“	“	
935	A. W.	31	5½	63	138	35	35–37½	24	“	“	“	“	
936	M. N.	38	11	69	195	41	41–43½	44	“	“	“	“	
937	F. H.	29	15	66	151	34½	34½–35½	36	“	“	“	“	
938	R. A.	26	3	65	150	32	32–34	34	“	“	“	“	
939	F. W.	27	6	68	161	36½	36½–39	30	“	“	“	“	
940	J. H.	33	4	67	164	26	36–38½	30	“	“	“	“	
941	E. M.	38	22	72	190	39	39–41	64	“	“	“	“	
942	J. E.	36	12	68	185	37	37–38½	30	“	“	“	“	
943	C. K.	41	8	71	196	38	38–40	32	“	“	“	“	
944	S.	34	12	69	157	35	35–37¾	50	“	“	“	“	
945	J. M.	25	8	66	164	34	34–36	36	“	“	“	“	
946	L. B.	34	2	71	184	35	35–37¾	30	“	“	“	“	
947	W. G.	33	6	70	190	36	36–38½	30	“	“	“	“	
948	O.	19	4	67½	160	34	34–35½	24	“	“	“	“	
949	A. S.	35	20	68	189	39	39–40½	30	“	“	“	“	
950	E. M.	27	2	68	178	37	37–39½	50	“	“	“	“	
951	F. G.	25	10	66	152	34	34–36½	50	“	“	“	“	
952	J. S.	33	12	64	135	35	35–36½	40	“	“	“	“	
953	J. S.*	39	23	66	148	34	34–36½	30	“	“	“	“	
954	G. L.	25	11	65	154	33	33–35	34	“	“	“	“	

Persons **employed** in S. **LIEBMANN** SONS' Brewery, examined **by** Dr. HUGO KOETHE, Brooklyn, E. D.—(*Continued.*)

No.	Initials of Persons Examined.	Age.	Length of Time Employed in Breweries—Years.	Height—Inches.	Weight—Lbs.	Circumference of Chest—Inches.	Difference in Forced Inspiration and Expiration.	Average Daily Consumption of Malt Beverages. Glasses.	General State of Health.	Condition of Liver.	Condition of Kidneys.	Condition of Heart.	SPECIAL REMARKS.
935	J. W.	28	4	66	165	34	34–36	30	Good.	Good.	Good.	Good.	
956	J. M.	26	2	68½	180	36	36–38½	50	"	"	"	"	
957	G.	46	20	66	162	36	36–38	50	"	"	"	"	
958	L.	22	8	66	170	36	36–39	40	"	"	"	"	
959	C. B.	23	2½	67	159	32	32–35½	30	"	"	"	"	
960	J. W.	22	8	67	166	37	37–40	30	"	"	"	"	
961	A. A.	21	2	64½	143	34	34–36	30	"	"	"	"	
962	J. R.	30	13	65½	163	34	34–36½	60	"	"	"	"	
963	N. B.	34	16	66½	157	34	34–36	20	"	"	"	"	
964	O.	39	18	66½	152	34	34–36	28	"	"	"	"	
965	C. W.	18	2½	70	160	32	32–34½	26	"	"	"	"	
966	M. S.	38	3	67½	173	36½	36½–38½	32	"	"	"	"	
967	G. F.	25	10	69½	170	34	34–36	86	"	"	"	"	
968	C. W.	18	½	70	183	34	34–36½	20	"	"	"	"	
969	B.	46	3	64	164	37	37–39	30	"	"	"	"	
970	C. G.	27	13	69	180	37	37–40	36	"	"	"	"	
971	J. B.	32	14	66	173	36	36–37½	30	"	"	"	"	
972	J. G.	45	32	71	228	41	41–43½	10	"	"	"	"	
973	J. B.	36	15	69½	208	39	39–41½	40	"	"	"	"	
974	R.	34	3½	67	164	35	35–37	40	"	"	"	"	
975	J. B.	39	15	67	174	36	36–39	30	"	"	"	"	
976	Z.	29	3	67½	195	37	37–38½	50	"	"	"	"	
977	A. G.	38	6	67	164	30	36–38½	40	"	"	"	"	
978	M. M.	45	12	67	178	36	36–38½	60	"	"	"	"	
979	K.	42	15	66	155	34	34–36	60	"	"	"	"	
980	B.	29	1½	68	158	37	37–38½	54	"	"	"	"	
981	F. L.	31	4½	73	240	40	40–42	60	"	"	"	"	
982	G. S.	32	16	67	245	42	42–44	20	"	"	"	"	
983	H.	29	3	72	188	35	35–38	40	"	"	"	"	
984	C. C.	26	1	71	188	37	37–39	50	"	"	"	"	
985	K.	29	4	67½	195	37	37–39½	60	"	"	"	"	
986	S.	28	5	67	165	36	36–38½	60	"	"	"	"	
987	P. M.	27	3	73	174	34	34–37	40	"	"	"	"	
988	B.	30	2½	69	169	34	34–36	20	"	"	"	"	
989	P. W.	22	3	66	183	37	37–40	50	"	"	"	"	
990	C. K.	35	6	64	164	36	36–38	40	"	"	"	"	
991	H.	21	1	66	162	34	34–37	40	"	"	"	"	
992	H.	30	4	67	156	34	34–37½	50	"	"	"	"	
993	J. M.	34	7	67	176	37	37–39	36	"	"	"	"	
994	J. B.	46	12	66	238	43	43–45	60	"	"	"	"	
995	G. W.	40	12	67	184	37	37–39½	50	"	"	"	"	
996	L. S.	23	4	70	210	36	36–38½	36	"	"	"	"	
997	J. W.	40	11	69	167	36	36–38½	40	"	"	"	"	
998	C. N.	38	8	70	190	37	37–39½	60	"	"	"	"	
999	J. F.	35	19	66	167	34	34–36½	60	"	"	"	"	
1000	A. H.	43	1	64	156	35	35–37	30	"	"	"	"	

www.ingramcontent.com/pod-product-compliance
Lightning Source LLC
Chambersburg PA
CBHW021436090426
42739CB00009B/1500